Filming Locations New York

200 ICONIC SCENES TO VISIT

ALEX CHILD

MUSEYON

NEW YORK

Library of Congress Cataloging-in-Publication Data

Names: Child, Alex, author.
Title: Filming locations New York : 200 iconic scenes to visit / Alex Child.
Description: New York : Museyon, 2018. | Includes filmography.
Identifiers: LCCN 2018038120 | ISBN 9781940842233 (hardcover : alk. paper)
Subjects: LCSH: Motion picture locations--New York (State)--New York.
Classification: LCC PN1993.5.U77 C455 2018 | DDC 917.47/10444--dc23
LC record available at https://lccn.loc.gov/2018038120

Published in the United States and Canada by:
Museyon, Inc.
333 E. 45th St.
New York, NY 10017

Museyon is a registered trademark.
Visit us online at www.museyon.com

ISBN 978-1-940842-23-3

Printed in China

Introduction/The Most Iconic Scenes of New York

New York City is one of the best backdrops for filmmakers.

The neighborhoods, landmarks, and buildings of New York City are recognized by people around the world through film and television. Directors know that setting their films and shows in the streets of New York adds value, so the city is always in demand by filmmakers. The cityscape appears in classics from *King Kong* to *Sex and the City*, like a character itself.

For New Yorkers, these films are a memoir of a lost New York. Every time I watch *Taxi Driver*, the tension and danger in the air and the revolting smell of Times Square in the 70s comes back to me. I feel the thrill that passes from the screen and it reminds me what life was like in the past. Good films inspire audiences in this way, even when watched over and over again.

Many New York classics such as *Midnight Cowboy*, *The Godfather*, *Annie Hall* and *Kramer vs. Kramer* won or were nominated for Oscars, Golden Globes and other awards. Directors like Martin Scorsese, Woody Allen and Spike Lee are known for their love of New York and their own versions of it. Film lovers can feel, empathize and appreciate their love and can't wait for their next releases.

In this book I chose 200 locations from well-loved films and TV shows. I hope you enjoy exploring the city with this book, whether you are just visiting or if you live in New York.

KING KONG (1933)

Here are my 10 favorite iconic scenes of New York. What are yours?

◆ *The Seven Year Itch* (1955, p.84): Marilyn Monroe's white dress is blown up by the breeze as she stands on the subway grate.

◆ *Manhattan* (1979, p.90): The silhouettes of Mary and Isaac sitting on a bench beneath the Queensboro Bridge at sunrise.

◆ *Taxi Driver* (1976, p.114): Travis walks through the filthy, seedy streets to the X-rated theater in Times Square.

◆ *Breakfast at Tiffany's* (1961, p.86): Holly Golightly eats her breakfast from a paper bag in front of Tiffany's window.

◆ *When Harry Met Sally...* (1989, p.162): As Sally and Harry sit at a table, Sally fakes an orgasm in Katz's Deli.

◆ *West Side Story* (1961, p.68): The opening scene, the rumble between two rival gangs, the Jets and the Sharks.

◆ *Midnight Cowboy* (1969, p.122): Rizzo screams, "I'm walkin' here! I'm walkin' here!" as a taxi almost hits him on Sixth Avenue.

◆ *Big* (1988, p.88): Tom Hanks as 12-year-old Josh and Mr. MacMillian play chopsticks on the walking piano at FAO Schwarz.

◆ *Serendipity* (2001, p.12): Jonathan and Sara have Frozen Hot Chocolate at Serendipity 3.

◆ *Leon: The Professional* (1994, p.124): Little Mathilda and Tony move from one hotel to another on Seventh Avenue.

Cheers!
Alex

Filming Locations New York

CONTENTS

200 ICONIC SCENES TO VISIT

*caption orders: clockwise from top left

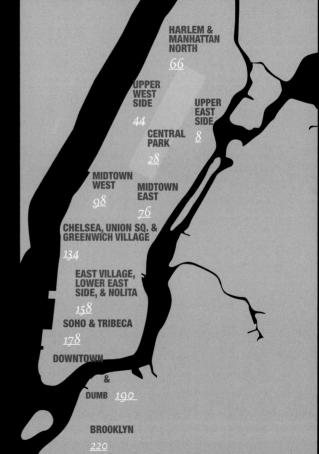

HARLEM & MANHATTAN NORTH

66

UPPER WEST SIDE

44

UPPER EAST SIDE

8

CENTRAL PARK

28

MIDTOWN WEST

98

MIDTOWN EAST

76

CHELSEA, UNION SQ. & GREENWICH VILLAGE

134

EAST VILLAGE, LOWER EAST SIDE, & NOLITA

158

SOHO & TRIBECA

178

DOWNTOWN & DUMB

190

BROOKLYN

220

UPPER
EAST
SIDE

BREAKFAST AT TIFFANY'S

SCENT OF A WOMAN (1992)

The Pierre Hotel: 2 East 61st Street

"Whoo-ah!" —*Lt. Col. Frank Slade*

A blind, retired army officer, Slade (Al Pacino), comes to New York with a prep school student, Charlie (Chris O'Donnell), who accepts a temporary job over Thanksgiving weekend to look after Slade. While waiting for drinks at an opulent hotel, Slade is captivated by Donna (Gabrielle Anwar), a beautiful young woman waiting for a date, because of the scent of her Ogilvie Sisters soap. A moment later, Slade leads her in a spectacular tango on the dance floor, surprising Charlie and everyone in the ballroom with his gracefulness. The tango scene was filmed at the grand ballroom of the Pierre Hotel, with the help of two choreographers, over four nights.

SERENDIPITY (2001)

Serendipity 3: 225 East 60th Street

"This is the ultimate blend to drink. How'd you find this place?" —*Jonathan*

Jonathan (John Cusack) meets Sara (Kate Beckinsale) while they both try to buy the last pair of black cashmere gloves at Bloomingdale's. Jonathan gallantly allows Sara to buy them, and she takes him to Serendipity 3 for Frozen Hot Chocolate in thanks. Even though they are both in relationships, they are attracted to each other, and decide to go ice skating at Wollman Rink in Central Park. As they part, they begin a game of fate to determine if they are meant to be together. Serendipity 3 opened in 1954. Regulars included Marilyn Monroe, Andy Warhol and even Jackie Kennedy. The First Lady once tried to buy the recipe for its famous Frozen Hot Chocolate, but the owner refused to give it to her.

03

ANNIE HALL (1977)

Annie Hall's Apartment: 68th Street between Madison and Park Avenues

"La-dee-da, la-dee-da, la-la." —*Annie Hall*

In one of the most iconic romantic comedies of all time, Alvy (Woody Allen) and Annie (Diane Keaton) first meet at a tennis court on a downtown pier. After the game she offers him a ride up to the Upper East Side, where they both live. Annie finds a parking spot on 68th Street near her apartment and the two have a brief exchange on the street, before she invites him up for a glass of wine. In the scene, the limestone buildings in the background capture the atmosphere of New York's Upper East Side, typical of Allen's films. While Annie Hall is one of film's most famous characters, her name, at least, isn't a work of fiction. Diane Keaton's real name is Diane Hall and her nickname is Annie.

04

MIDNIGHT COWBOY (1969)

68th Street and Park Avenue: Cass's Apartment, 114 East 72nd Street

"I'm new here in town. Just in from Texas, you know…and I'm looking for the Statue of Liberty." —*Joe Buck*

Joe Buck (John Voight) arrives in New York from Texas in hopes of making it big as a gigolo. He begins wandering the city streets dressed like a rodeo cowboy looking for women to hustle. On Park Avenue on the Upper East Side, he asks a wealthy-looking woman for directions to the Statue of Liberty, but his attempt to pick her up fails. When he is finally successful in bedding a middle-aged woman, Cass (Sylvia Miles), she cons him into giving her $20 instead. Miles received an Oscar nomination for her brief appearance as a manic

New York City call girl. "Do it for Mama!" Later he meets the equally hard-on-his-luck "Ratso" Rizzo (Dustin Hoffman) at a bar.

05

THE THOMAS CROWN AFFAIR (1999)

The Metropolitan Museum of Art: Fifth Avenue and 82nd Street

"Do you want to dance? Or do you want to DANCE?"
—*Thomas Crown*

A bored billionaire, Thomas Crown (Pierce Brosnan), orchestrates an elaborate heist to steal a painting by Claude Monet from the Metropolitan Museum of Art. While insurance investigator Catherine (Rene Russo) suspects and chases Crown, her interest turns romantic. Crown decides to return the painting under the eyes of Catherine and dozens of police officers to prove his sincerity and test her loyalty to him. The painting at the center of the film, *San Giorgio Maggiore at Dusk*, is actually owned by The National Museum and Art Gallery, Cardiff, Wales. Although the exterior of the museum was portrayed by the Met, interior scenes were filmed at the New York Public Library and on a soundstage.

INTERNATIONAL (2009)

R. Guggenheim Museum: Fifth Avenue and 88th Street

**imes the hardest thing in life is to know which bridge to cross
hich to burn . . . I'm the one you burn." —*Louis***

following Interpol agent, Louis (Clive
en) and Manhattan assistant district
Eleanor (Naomi Watts) through New
nbul, Milan and Berlin as they try to
he crimes of an international bank, the
shootout scene, takes place inside the
ggenheim Museum. The bank's agents
ouis, riddling the museum with bullet
uis fires back, hitting the skylight. The
r shatters, the skylight crashes down,

bullet holes in the Guggenheim—the shootout
was filmed in a replica of the interior that was
built to scale by Babelsberg Studios in Germany.

UPPER EAST SIDE

01 SCENT OF A WOMAN (1992)

The Pierre Hotel: 2 East 61st Street

Slade leads Donna in a spectacular tango on the dance floor of the hotel's magnificent grand ballroom.

02 SERENDIPITY (2001)

Serendipity 3: 225 East 60th Street

Sara thanks Jonathan by inviting him to Serendipity 3 for a Frozen Hot Chocolate, the restaurant's speciality.

03 ANNIE HALL (1977)

Annie Hall's Apartment: 68th Street and Madison Avenue

Annie finds a parking spot near her apartment, on beautiful, brownstone filled, East 68th Street.

04 MIDNIGHT COWBOY (1969)

68th Street and Park Avenue

Joe searches for wealthy women on Park Avenue, hoping to turn them into customers, when he meets Cass.

05 THE THOMAS CROWN AFFAIR (1999)

The Metropolitan Museum of Art

Bored billionaire Thomas Crown orchestrates an elaborate heist and steals a Monet from the museum.

06 THE INTERNATIONAL (1999)

Solomon R. Guggenheim Museum: 1071 Fifth Avenue

An action-packed shootout between Louis and the bank's agents takes place in the distinctive curves of the museum.

07 SPLASH (1984)

Bloomingdale's: 59th Street and Lexington Avenue

Allen finds the mermaid, Madison, in Bloomies with a new wardrobe, and also discovers that she is able to talk.

08 THE SEVEN YEAR ITCH (1955)

Richard's Apartment: 164 East 61st Street

Richard meets his stunning neighbor, a 22-year-old blonde model, who is renting the apartment directly above him.

09 SIX DEGREES OF SEPARATION (1993)

Kittredges' Apartment: 860 Fifth Avenue

Art dealers Ouisa and Flan are visited one evening by a young man, Paul, who claims to be a friend of their children.

10 BREAKFAST AT TIFFANY'S (1961)

Holly's Apartment: 169 East 71st Street

One morning Holly is awakened by new tenant Paul Varjak ringing the doorbell, and their romance begins.

UPPER EAST SIDE

11 **THE PRINCE OF TIDES (1991)**

Susan's Office: 4 East 74th Street

After his twin sister Savannah's suicide attempt, Tom travels to New York to meet his sister's psychiatrist, Susan.

12 **HANNAH AND HER SISTERS (1986)**

Café Carlyle: 35 East 76th Street

Mickey takes his ex-wife's sister, the cocaine-snorting Holly, to listen to Bobby Short here. He loves it, she hates it.

13 **CRUEL INTENTIONS (1999)**

Valmont Mansion: 2 East 79th Street

Kathryn and her step-brother Sebastian live in the lavish French Gothic-style mansion, the Harry F. Sinclair House.

14 **BUTTERFIELD 8 (1960)**

Liggett's Apartment: 1050 Fifth Avenue

After her lover leaves, Gloria finds a note with $250 cash. She furiously scrawls "No Sale" on the living room mirror.

15 **WORKING GIRL (1988)**

Carnegie Mansion: 2 East 91st Street

Tess and Jack crash Oren Trask's daughter's wedding, the only chance they'll have to pitch their business plan.

16 **A PERFECT MURDER (1998)**

Steve & Emily Taylor's Apartment: 1 East 91st Street

Steven meets with David to reveal his true identity, and then offers him $500,000 in cash to murder his wife.

17 **25TH HOUR (2002)**

Carl Schurz Park

Monty sits in the park with Doyle, the dog he rescued, on his last day of freedom before serving a prison sentence.

18 **SEX AND THE CITY (1998–2004)**

Barneys New York: 660 Madison Avenue

After Charlotte decides to volunteer to help the blind, she tries walking through Barneys while blindfolded.

19 **SEX AND THE CITY (1998–2004)**

Stanhope Hotel: 995 Fifth Avenue

As Aidan is refinishing the floors in Carrie's apartment, she stays at the Stanhope, where she and Big begin their affair.

20 **SEX AND THE CITY: THE MOVIE (2008)**

Carrie and Big's Apartment: 1030 Fifth Avenue

Carrie and Big live in a "little more down-to-earth" apartment on the 12th floor.

CENTRAL PARK

THE APRIL FOOLS (1969)

21

DEFINITELY, MAYBE (2008)

The Pond

"Did you know that 35 people try to jump off the Brooklyn Bridge each year, most because of broken hearts?" —*Maya*

When his college sweetheart Emily (Elizabeth Banks) visits him in New York, Will (Ryan Reynolds) proposes while walking in Central Park. She responds by confessing that she slept with his roommate, saying that she is "letting him go" because she is not able to share his career ambitions. In the film, the incident is one of the romantic adventures Will recalls for his young daughter Maya (Abigail Breslin), who asks him about his life before marriage. Although Will is in the midst of a divorce, he finds that a second look at the past may give him a second chance at the future. Nonetheless Will is a lucky guy, who is loved by four (including daughter Maya) beautiful and witty girls!

KRAMER VS. KRAMER (1979)

The Mall, Central Park

"I am not going to say it again. I am not going to say it again." —*Ted*

Since the Kramer family lives on the Upper East Side, Central Park is Billy's (Justin Henry) playground. The park's tree-lined Mall appears twice in the film. In the summer, Billy tries to ride a bicycle for the first time with help from his father, Ted (Dustin Hoffman). Billy later sees his mother Joanna (Meryl Streep) in winter, fifteen months after she has left the family. The film swept the Academy Awards in 1979 and became an important milestone in the careers of both Dustin Hoffman and Meryl Streep. Did you know that the famous ice cream scene, where Billy challenges his father by skipping dinner and going straight for dessert, was completely improvised by both Dustin Hoffman and Justin Henry?

WHEN HARRY MET SALL

SCENES IN CENTRAL PARK

SERENDIPITY (2001)
FRIENDS WITH BENEFITS (2011)
IT SHOULD HAPPEN TO YOU
(1954)
THE AVENGERS (2012)

23

IT COULD HAPPEN TO YOU (1994)

Bethesda Terrace, Central Park

Yvonne: "Because of me, you have nothing."
Charlie: "Because of you, I have you."

Inspired by the true story of a New York police officer who split a $6 million lottery win with a waitress, this film tells the story of police officer Charlie (Nicolas Cage), who, when left without enough cash to tip his waitress at a diner, promises to split his lottery ticket as a tip. When the ticket wins big, the lives of Charlie and the bankrupted waitress Yvonne (Bridget Fonda) are drastically changed. The pair rollerblades at Bethesda Terrace in Central Park when Charlie plunges into a pond, and they begin falling in love as their lives fall apart around them. Charlie says, "I told you I'd share my ticket. I never planned on sharing my heart."

24

CAFÉ SOCIETY (2016)

Bow Bridge, Central Park

"Life is a comedy written by a sadistic comedy writer." —*Bobby*

Café Society, Woody Allen's 46th film, is a 1930's tale of Hollywood glamour and New York nightlife. After Bobby (Jesse Eisenberg) loses his love Vonnie (Kristen Stewart) he returns to New York from LA, runs a nightclub and is swept up in the world of café society. Bobby is surprised when Phil (Steve Carrell) and Vonnie, now married, visit New York and show up at the nightclub. Bobby and Vonnie decide to tour the city. They spend a day together, and kiss on the Bow Bridge in Central Park. The New York nightclub scenes were actually filmed on a set inspired by a combination of places that production designer Loquasto and Allen visited, even with a touch of the 1930s El Morocco, famous for its blue zebra-stripe motif.

CENTRAL PARK

21 DEFINITELY, MAYBE (2007)

The Pond

Will proposes to Emily in Central Park, but she turns him down, confessing that she slept with his old roommate.

22 KRAMER VS. KRAMER (1979)

The Mall

Ted teaches Billy to ride a bicycle for the first time at the Mall in the middle of Central Park.

23 IT COULD HAPPEN TO YOU (1994)

Bethesda Terrace

Charlie and Yvonne have fun rollerblading here before he plunges into the pond.

24 CAFÉ SOCIETY (2016)

Bow Bridge

Bobby agrees to show Vonnie around New York. They spend a day together, leading up to a kiss on a bridge in the park.

25 MADAGASCAR (2005)

Central Park Zoo

Alex, Marty, Melman, and Gloria leave the zoo and get shipwrecked on the island of Madagascar.

26 LOVE STORY (1970)

Wollman Rink

The doomed couple enjoys a romantic day. Jennifer longingly watches Oliver skate at the rink.

27 WALL STREET (1987)

Sheep Meadow

Bud, wearing a wire to record evidence of insider trading, confronts Gordon Gekko in rainy Central Park.

28 BREAKFAST AT TIFFANY'S (1961)

Naumburg Bandshell

Fred wants Paul's help to get his wife back, not knowing that Paul is falling in love with Holly.

29 MARATHON MAN (1976)

The Reservoir

'Babe' Levy trains on the 1.6 mile jogging path that surrounds the reservoir in Central Park.

30 SEX AND THE CITY (1998–2004)

The Loeb Boathouse

In one of the series' funniest scenes, Mr. Big and Carrie meet for lunch here, and they end up falling in the pond.

25

26

27

29

30

THE PRODUCERS (2005)

UPPER
WEST
SIDE

THE APARTMENT (1960)

GHOSTBUSTERS (1984)

Columbus Circle

"I tried to think of the most harmless thing...something that could never, ever possibly destroy us —Mr. Stay Puft!"
—Dr. Raymond Stanz

You can't help laughing when Ray (Dan Aykroyd) says "I couldn't help it. It just popped in there." At the climax, the Marshmallow Man, one of two physical bodies of Gozer, appears on Broadway and 57th Street and then lumbers up Columbus Circle, causing cars to crash and scaring the crowds, to the Gozer's building (55 Central Park West). Dr. Venkman (Bill Murray) says "We've been going about this all wrong. This Mr. Stay Puft's okay! He's a sailor, he's in New York; we get this guy laid, we won't have any trouble!" Did you know that Mr. Stay Puft, a fictional character that looks like the Michelin Man and the Pillsbury Doughboy, was conceived by Dan Aykroyd?

CROCODILE DUNDEE (1986)

Columbus Circle Subway Station

"That's incredible. Imagine seven million people all wanting to live together. Yeah, New York must be the friendliest place on earth." —*Dundee*

The music swells as reporter Sue (Linda Kozlowski) takes off her shoes and runs down to the platform of the Columbus Circle subway station to find her former subject Mick Dundee (Paul Hogan) standing far beyond the crowd. Calling out to Sue, "I'm coming through," Dundee walks on the heads of the cheering crowds to reach his beloved. In a case of life imitating art, Linda Kozlowski and Paul Hogan actually married after the film. This memorable final-scene love confession was filmed on the same abandoned platform of Brooklyn's Hoyt–Schermerhorn subway station as Michael Jackson's "Bad."

MOONSTRUCK (1987)

Lincoln Center: 63rd Street and Columbus Avenue

"Snap out of it!" —*Loretta*

One full-moon night, Loretta (Cher), a newly engaged Italian-American widow, sets out to share the news with her fiancé's estranged brother Ronny (Nicolas Cage). After a long, passionate conversation, the two end up in bed together. Although she feels ashamed the following morning, Loretta agrees to go to the opera with him that night, provided they never see each other again. She stops at church for confession, goes to a beauty salon to get her hair done and buys a new dress and shoes. Transformed, Loretta and Ronny meet at the fountain at Lincoln Center and she enjoys her first opera, *La Bohème*. Not long after Loretta's

fiancé returns from visiting his mother in Italy, they all end up toasting her engagement to his brother Ronny. "Alla famiglia!"

34

ROSEMARY'S BABY (1987)

The Dakota: 1 West 72nd Street

"This isn't a dream! This is really happening!" —*Rosemary*

The frightening tale opens showing the Upper East Side from Central Park West, then focuses on the Dakota (named The Bramford), as Rosemary (Mia Farrow) and Guy (John Cassavetes) meet a real estate broker at the building's entrance. Ira Levin, the author of the book, was inspired by Alwyn Court (180 West 58th Street), but director Roman Polanski set the film at the Dakota. The film gave the Dakota a reputation as "haunted and cursed," but it was the first luxury apartment house in America and little changed. Celebrities have called it home, including Boris Karloff, Leonard Bernstein, Lauren Bacall, Rosemary Clooney,

John Lennon and Yoko Ono. Lauren Bacall's 4,000-square-foot residence sold for $21 million in 2015. Wouldn't you want to live there — even sharing a room with Satan?

35

SINGLE WHITE FEMALE (1992)

The Ansonia: 2109 Broadway at 73rd Street

"SWF seeks female to share apartment in west 70s. Non-smoker professional preferred." —*Allie*

After breaking up with her boyfriend, Allie (Bridget Fonda) advertises for a roommate. She eventually settles on Hedra (Jennifer Jason Leigh), but soon finds her new roommate's horrifying true nature, as Hedra begins taking on aspects of Allie's personality. The apartment building where the thriller unfolds is itself another star of the film, its façade and stairwells played by the Ansonia on the Upper West Side. It was built as a luxury residential hotel in 1899 in the lavish Beaux-Arts style. Many celebrated residents have called the Ansonia home, including Babe Ruth, Igor Stravinsky, and Angelina Jolie.

YOU'VE GOT MAIL (1998)

Zabar's: 2245 Broadway at 80th Street

"When you read a book as a child, it becomes a part of your identity in a way that no other reading in your whole life does."
—Kathleen

On Thanksgiving Day, Kathleen (Meg Ryan) goes shopping and mistakenly ducks into the cash-only line at Zabar's, a gourmet food store, to hide from her business competitor, Joe (Tom Hanks). Surprisingly, Joe helps Kathleen deal with a difficult cashier and heckling customers, without the two realizing that they have been flirting via e-mail. Like many of the locations in the film, Zabar's is an Upper West Side institution, and the film paints a charming picture of the neighborhood. Other true-to-life locations include the characters' apartments, hot-dog stand Gray's Papaya, the romantic Café Lalo and the 91st Street Garden in Riverside Park.

NIGHT AT THE MUSEUM (2006)

American Museum of Natural History: 79th Street and Central Park West

"Ok, Attila the Hun: What is that guy's problem?" —*Larry*

Based on the 1993 children's book *The Night at the Museum* by Milan Trenc, the film tells the story of a divorced father, Larry (Ben Stiller), who takes a job as a night watchman at the American Museum of Natural History to impress his son. Larry discovers the exhibits come to life at night, making him responsible for a rambunctious tyrannosaurus skeleton nicknamed Rexy, as well as the cowboy Jedediah (Owen Wilson) and his nemesis, the Roman general Octavius (Steve Coogan). While internal scenes of the museum were filmed at a sound stage in Vancouver, children and the young at heart will find plenty of magic among the museum's diorama displays.

UPPER WEST SIDE

31 GHOSTBUSTERS (1984)
Columbus Circle: 59th Street and Broadway
Gozer's destructor, the giant Marshmallow Man, frightens the city as he lumbers through Columbus Circle.

32 CROCODILE DUNDEE (1986)
Columbus Circle Subway Station
Sue and Mick exchange loving looks through the crowd while waiting for a train.

33 MOONSTRUCK (1987)
Lincoln Center
Loretta and Ronny meet at the fountain at Lincoln Center on their way to see the opera *La Bohème*.

34 ROSEMARY'S BABY (1968)
The Dakota: 1 West 72nd Street
Rosemary and Guy move into an antiquated New York apartment building with mysterious neighbors.

35 SINGLE WHITE FEMALE (1992)
The Ansonia: 2109 Broadway
Allie searches for a roommate after separating from her boyfriend, and she decides to let Hedra move in.

36 YOU'VE GOT MAIL (1998)
Zabar's: 2245 Broadway
Kathleen mistakenly stands in a cash-only line at Zabar's, and Joe steps in to save her from the surly cashier.

37 NIGHT AT THE MUSEUM (2006)
American Museum of Natural History
Larry takes a job as a night watchman at the museum to impress his 10-year-old son Nick.

38 GHOSTBUSTERS (1984)
Gozer's Building: 15 Central Park West
Dana and Louis live in the building built as a gateway to summon the ancient and evil Gozer.

39 THE FIRST WIVES CLUB (1996)
Leopard at des Artistes: 1 West 67th Street
After Cynthia's funeral, Brenda, Elise, and Annie have lunch together, reuniting for the first time since college.

40 NEW YORK STORIES (1989)
Tavern on the Green: Central Park West and 67th Street
In the "Oedipus Wrecks" sequence Sheldon has dinner with his mother, fiancée, Lisa and her children at the restaurant.

UPPER WEST SIDE

THE APARTMENT (1960)

CC Baxter's Apartment: 55 West 69th Street

CC Baxter tries to rise in the ranks of his company by letting its executives use his apartment for trysts near Central Park.

WHEN HARRY MET SALLY... (1989)

Cafe Luxembourg: 200 West 70th Street

Marie states that "restaurants are to people in the '80s what theater was to people in the '60s."

DIE HARD WITH A VENGEANCE (1995)

72nd Street Subway Station

Simon instructs McClane and Carver to travel to the Wall Street Station within 30 minutes.

GREEN CARD (1990)

Bronte's Apartment: 60 West 76th Street

Following her attorney's advice, Brontë reluctantly invites Georges to move into her apartment.

HEARTBURN (1986)

Rachel's Apartment: 2211 Broadway

Rachel moves back to NYC and in with her father, and attempts to get her job back as a food writer.

YOU'VE GOT MAIL (1998)

Café Lalo: 201 West 83rd Street

"Shopgirl" (Kathleen) waits for "NY152" (Joe) to meet at the European-style café, while Joe's friends peek in the window.

KISSING JESSICA STEIN (2001)

Jessica's Apartment: 61 West 88th Street

Jessica lives in an Upper West Side apartment that is crammed with books and has a spiral staircase.

YOU'VE GOT MAIL (1998)

Riverside Park: 91st Street Garden

When Kathleen sees Joe in the garden, she realizes he is her on-line friend, and she says, "I wanted it to be you so badly!"

SEX AND THE CITY (1998–2004)

Columbus Circle Fountains

With the fountains as a backdrop, Carrie and Aidan realize their relationship is not going to work.

SEX AND THE CITY: THE MOVIE 2 (2010)

Empire Hotel: 44 West 63rd Street

Carrie catches her husband, Mr. Big flirting with Carmen, a banker, at a hotel bar.

HARLEM & MANHATTAN NORTH

KLUTE (1971)

WEST SIDE STORY (1961)

Playground: 110th Street Between Second and Third Avenues

"Beat it!" —*Riff, the leader of the Jets*

Winning 10 Academy Awards including Best Picture, *West Side Story* is one of the most loved musicals in movie history. The updated New York version of Romeo and Juliet is told through the lives of two Upper West Side gangs, the Jets and the Sharks. The opening prologue that begins with finger snapping is a montage of dance scenes at the playground on East 110th Street and at West 68th Street (between Amsterdam and West End Avenue). The tenement buildings that appear in the background on West 68th Street were torn down and became the Lincoln Towers complex. Did you notice the scene where some gang members have encroached on rival territory with the emphatic line, "beat it" in the opening? Was Michael Jackson inspired by the famous "Beat It" from *West Side Story*?

MALCOLM X (1992)

Apollo Theater: 253 West 125th Street

"We didn't land on Plymouth Rock—Plymouth Rock landed on us." —*Malcolm X*

The scene where Malcolm X (Denzel Washington) speaks in front of the African Bookstore on 125th Street was based on a photo and filmed on a set at Third Avenue between 118th and 121st streets, showing landmarks such as the Apollo Theater. The Apollo's marquee indicates the date, even though Sarah Vaughan's name is misspelled as "Vaughn." Washington was nominated for an Academy Award for Best Actor. To prepare, he interviewed Malcolm X's wife and two of his brothers, avoided eating pork, attended Fruit of Islam classes and learned to Lindy Hop. Annoyed by Washington's loss to Al Pacino for *Scent of a Woman*, the director Spike Lee said, "I'm not the only one who thinks Denzel was robbed on that one."

HARLEM & MANHATTAN NORTH

51 WEST SIDE STORY (1961)

110th Street between Second and Third Avenues

Two Upper West Side gangs, the Jets and the Sharks encroach on rival territory.

52 MALCOLM X (1992)

Apollo Theater: 253 West 125th Street

Malcolm X gives a speech in front of the African Bookstore and the iconic Harlem Theater on 125th Street.

53 SEINFELD (1989–1998)

Monk's Café (Tom's Restaurant): 2880 Broadway

The gang regularly meets at this typical NYC diner, a favorite for Jerry's egg-white omelette and Elaine's big salad.

54 SPIDER-MAN (2002)

Columbia University

Peter visits a genetics laboratory where he is bitten by a super spider, giving him superhuman powers.

55 SPIDER-MAN 2 (2004)

Riverside Church: 490 Riverside Drive

Mary Jane is about to be married to astronaut John Jameson, but she leaves him at the altar for Peter.

56 THE LAST SEDUCTION (1994)

Bridget's Apartment: 45 Tiemann Place

Bridget steals the money her husband made from selling cocaine, and flees their apartment while he is in the shower.

57 AMERICAN GANGSTER (2007)

Mount Olivet Baptist Church: 201 Malcolm X Boulevard

Frank is arrested as he emerges from a service at the church where he was married earlier.

58 JUNGLE FEVER (1991)

Sylvia's Restaurant: 328 Malcolm X Boulevard

Flipper and Angie get an attitude from the waitress (played by Queen Latifah) at the famous soul food restaurant.

59 JUNGLE FEVER (1991)

Purify's House: 252 West 139th Street (Strivers' Row)

Successful and happily married Purify lives in the historic house with his wife Brew and daughter Ming.

60 THE ROYAL TENENBAUMS (2001)

The Tenenbaum House: 444 West 144th Street

At Henry and Etheline's wedding, Eli crashes his car into the side of the house.

53

53

56

54

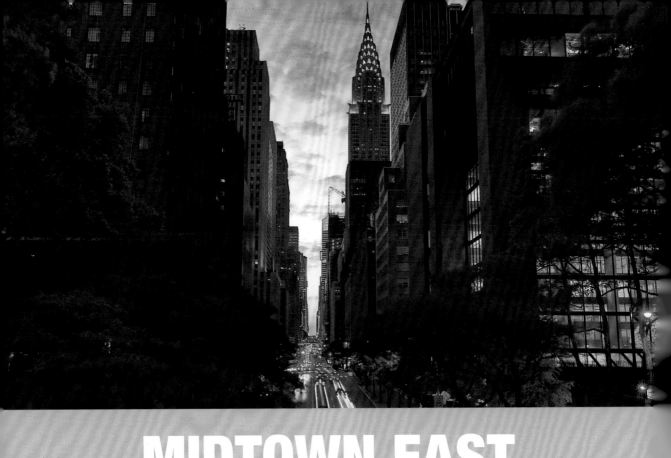

MIDTOWN EAST

HOW TO MARRY A MILLIONAIRE (1953)

THE FISHER KING (1991)

Grand Central Terminal

"There's three things in this world that you need: Respect for all kinds of life, a nice bowel movement on a regular basis, and a navy blazer." —*Parry*

Jack (Jeff Bridges) and Parry (Robin Williams) come to Grand Central Terminal to see Lydia (Amanda Plummer), with whom Parry is smitten. At five minutes before 5 p.m. she appears in the crowded station and Parry follows her. Suddenly the commuters start waltzing in the main hall. This magical scene was filmed between 3 a.m. and 5 a.m. with 400 extras who took hours of waltz lessons for this urgent change in the script. The director, Terry Gilliam, later said, "I think the Grand Central Station waltz sequence in *The Fisher King* is

as good as anything I've done." The Terminal was actually turned into a big dance hall for the Centennial Celebration on February 1, 2013.

62

THE INTERPRETER (2005)

United Nations, General Assembly

"Countries have gone to war because they've misinterpreted one another. " —*Silvia*

Sydney Pollack's final film was the first ever filmed inside of the United Nations—and it took a direct appeal from the director to then U.N. Secretary-General Kofi Annan to get permission to film there. In the film, Nicole Kidman stars as Silvia, an interpreter at the General Assembly who is forced to become involved in a plan to assassinate the president of the African nation of Matobo. The nearby Dag Hammarskjöld Plaza is named for the organization's second Secretary-General, who died in a mysterious plane crash while mediating Congo's independence—perhaps the most famous real-life case of intrigue involving the U.N. and Africa. Guided tours of the United Nations are available Monday through Friday.

THE SEVEN YEAR ITCH (1955)

Lexington Avenue between 51st and 52nd Streets

"Oh, do you feel the breeze from the subway? Isn't it delicious?" —*The "Girl"*

Having just seen *Creature from the Black Lagoon*, an unnamed girl (Marilyn Monroe) and Richard (Tom Ewell) come out from the Trans-Lux Theatre on a hot summer's day. She stands over a subway gate as the breeze from the train blows her white dress up around her legs. The scene was filmed on location early on the morning of September 15, 1954, with thousands of excited fans crowded nearby. A second take was shot on a sound stage at the 20th Century Fox lot. While the image of Monroe with her dress billowing around her is one of the most iconic images of the 20th century, the film actually only shows her legs cut with reaction shots, never in full-length like the famous image.

BREAKFAST AT TIFFANY'S (1961)

Tiffany & Company, 727 Fifth Avenue

Paul: "So what? So plenty! I love you, you belong to me!"
Holly: "No. People don't belong to people."

Early one morning, a yellow cab pulls over at Tiffany's on Fifth Avenue. "Moon River" plays in the background, as the car approaches from the south (in reality Fifth Avenue runs in the opposite direction). Dressed in pearls and a black Givenchy gown, Holly Golightly (Audrey Hepburn) steps out onto the street and nibbles a pastry and sips coffee while window-shopping at the iconic jeweler. Today it is one of film's most famous scenes, but it could have turned out very differently. Instead of the gamine Hepburn, the part was first offered to the bombshell Marilyn Monroe.

BIG (1988)

Apple Store (FAO Schwarz): 767 Fifth Avenue at 58th Street

Josh: "Do you mean sleep over?" *Susan*: "Well, yeah." *Josh*: "OK…but I get to be on top."

The famous scene where Josh (Tom Hanks), a 12-year-old boy trapped in the body of a 30-year-old man, and toy magnate Mr. MacMillan (Robert Loggia) play "Heart and Soul" and "Chopsticks" on a giant piano was filmed at the FAO Schwarz toy store. On the day of filming, stuntmen were on hand just in case the two could not do the dance moves correctly, but the actors were determined to do the entire keyboard number without the aid of the stuntmen. They succeeded. Shoppers can still dance on the legendary Big Piano on the One Below floor of Macy's on 34th Street—or take it home with them for $250,000.

MANHATTAN (1979)

58th Street & the East River, Sutton Place

"Boy, this is really a great city, I don't care what anybody says— it's really a knock-out, you know?" —*Isaac*

When Isaac (Woody Allen), a 42-year-old TV writer, meets Mary (Diane Keaton), a mistress of his best friend, he initially thinks she's a snob. But then he runs into her again at a party at the Museum of Modern Art and shares a cab ride home with her. They walk her dog and chat until sunrise at the East River, where they realize they get along better than they originally thought. The iconic scene of the couple's silhouettes under the Queensboro Bridge, while George Gershwin's "Someone to Watch Over Me" plays in the background, is one of the most beloved moments in New York City film history. It wasn't an easy shot to get, however. The scene was filmed at 5 a.m., and required the crew to bring their own bench.

MIDTOWN EAST

61 THE FISHER KING (1991)

Grand Central Terminal

While Parry follows Lydia, the commuters begin to magically pair up and waltz in the main hall.

62 THE INTERPRETER (2005)

The United Nations, General Assembly

Silvia overhears a plan, and is then forced to get involved in the plan to assassinate the president of Matobo.

63 THE SEVEN YEAR ITCH (1955)

Lexington Avenue at 52nd Street

The setting of the famous image of Marilyn Monroe standing on the subway grate as her dress is blown up by the breeze.

64 BREAKFAST AT TIFFANY'S (1961)

Tiffany & Co., 727 Fifth Avenue

Holly eats a pastry and drinks coffee while window-shopping in her famous little black dress, designed by Givenchy.

65 BIG (1988)

Apple Store at 767 Fifth Avenue

Josh and Mr. MacMillan play "Heart and Soul" and "Chopsticks" by dancing on the keys of a giant piano.

66 MANHATTAN (1979)

58th Street & The East River, Sutton Place

Isaac and Mary chat until sunrise at the East River, and the image was so striking it was chosen for the film's poster.

67 MEN IN BLACK 3 (2012)

The Chrysler Building

In order to save Agent K, J jumps from the building to travel back to 1969.

68 SUPERMAN (1978)

The Daily Planet: 220 East 42nd Street

Clark Kent is a reporter at the newspaper the *Daily Planet,* located in an Art Deco building in Metropolis.

69 SCARFACE (1983)

Tudor City

Tony tries to assassinate a Bolivian journalist by planting a bomb in the journalist's car.

70 MAN ON A LEDGE (2012)

The Roosevelt Hotel

Nick climbs on the ledge from his room on the 21st floor and threatens to jump.

MIDTOWN EAST

71 SERENDIPITY (2001)

The Waldorf Astoria Hotel

Sara and Jonathan test their fate in the hotel elevators, but still end up finding each other.

72 ARTHUR (1981)

St. Bartholomew's Church: 109 East 50th Street

Arthur arrives at the church drunk, cancels his wedding, and gets beat up by the bride's angry father.

73 THE DEVIL WEARS PRADA (2006)

Smith & Wollensky: 797 Third Avenue

Andy runs to the famous steakhouse to get her boss, the editor-in-chief of *Runway* magazine, a steak for lunch.

74 GOSSIP GIRL (2007-2012)

The Palace Hotel: 455 Madison Avenue

Bart, Chuck's father, owns the hotel and lives with his new wife Lily van der Woodsen and her children Serena and Eric.

75 THE LOST WEEKEND (1945)

P. J. Clarke's: 913 Third Avenue

Don, an alcoholic writer, decides to sell his typewriter for money for booze, and then he's refused service at Nat's Bar.

76 MISS CONGENIALITY (2000)

St. Regis Hotel: 2 East 55th Street

Beauty pageant coach Victor meets Gracie and begins to coach her on how to dress, walk, and behave like a contestant.

77 THE DEVIL'S ADVOCATE (1997)

Trump Tower: 725 Fifth Avenue

Kevin investigates the murder of billionaire Alex Cullen and meets him at his lavish residence (Donald Trump's penthouse).

78 HOW TO MARRY A MILLIONAIRE (1953)

Sutton Place Penthouse: 36 Sutton Place South

New York models, Schatze, Pola and Loco sublet a palatial penthouse hoping to attract and marry millionaires.

79 SEX AND THE CITY (1998−2004)

Monkey Bar: 60 East 54th Street

Carrie and Mr. Big go to see a jazz show at the bar, but then Carrie meets one of the musicians, Ray.

80 SEX AND THE CITY (1998−2004)

Tao: 42 East 58th Street

In an awkward unplanned date, Mr. Big shows up with a supermodel, while Carrie is with Ray, the jazz musician.

MIDTOWN
WEST

AN AFFAIR TO REMEMBER (1957)

SLEEPLESS IN SEATTLE (1993)

Empire State Building: 350 Fifth Avenue at 34th Street

"I am not going to New York to meet some woman who could be a crazy, sick lunatic! Didn't you see *Fatal Attraction*?" —*Sam*

The film was inspired by *An Affair to Remember* (1957), considered one of the most romantic films of all time according to the American Film Institute. Although Cary Grant and Deborah Kerr never met on the top of the Empire State Building in the original, Sam (Tom Hanks) and Annie (Meg Ryan) do make it there on Valentine's Day, with the help of Sam's son Jonah (Ross Malinger) in the film's final scene. You can recreate the scene yourself with a visit to the skyscraper's observation deck, 1,250 feet above the city. Did you know that the scene was filmed on a Seattle set that had been made to look like the observation deck of the Empire State Building?

82

MIRACLE ON 34TH STREET (1996)

Macy's: 151 West 34th Street

"Oh... one of those. I don't know any of those. My mother thinks they're silly." —*Susan*

Every year when Christmas Day approaches, I can't help watching this classic holiday tale, and I especially enjoy the real scenes of old New York. Maureen O'Hara (as Doris Walker) said, "Those sequences, like the one with Kris Kringle (Edmund Gwenn) riding in the sleigh and waving to the cheering crowd, were real-life moments in the 1946 Macy's Parade." The little girl at the heart of the story, Susan (played by 8-year-old Natalie Wood), doesn't believe in Santa at first, because her mom, Doris, has raised her as a realist. But the happy ending, and the miracle that occurs, makes us all

believers! Don't miss sweet little Natalie Wood; she was so young while filming that she really did still believe in Santa.

SEX AND THE CITY: THE MOVIE (2008)

New York Public Library: 476 Fifth Avenue

"Are you the last person in New York still taking out library books?" —*Mr. Big*

When newspaper columnist Carrie Bradshaw (Sarah Jessica Parker) visits the New York Public Library to return the book *Love Letters of Great Men*, she decides it would be the perfect venue for her wedding to her longtime off-and-on paramour, Mr. Big (Chris Noth). But on the big day, an overwhelmed Big has second thoughts. Devastated, Carrie flees the wedding and attacks Big with her bouquet on 40th Street between Fifth and Sixth avenues, adjacent to Bryant Park. In reality, Carrie would have never returned a book here; the Schwarzman Building is a research facility. The lending library branch is across the street.

ONE FINE DAY (1996)

Circle Line Sightseeing Cruises: Pier 83 at West 42nd Street

"That's one of the advantages of being an adult. You get to act like a kid anytime you feel like it." —*Jack*

When Maggie and Sammy miss their school field trip on the Circle Line at Pier 83, Maggie's divorced dad, reporter Jack (George Clooney), and Sammy's divorced mom, architect Melanie (Michelle Pfeiffer), are forced to supervise each other's kids for the day. As they balance the demands of their careers and children, Jack and Melanie run around the city. After such a hectic day, is it any surprise that the two quickly fall asleep on the couch at Melanie's house? Did you know that the popular Circle Line Sightseeing Cruise completely circles Manhattan, passing under 20 bridges and passes by more than 130 of the city's most iconic landmarks and has been in business since 1945?

85

BIRDMAN OR (THE UNEXPECTED VIRTUE OF IGNORANCE) (2014) *St. James Theatre: 246 West 44th Street*

"Popularity is the slutty little cousin of prestige." —*Mike*

The film was shot at Broadway's St. James Theatre and at Kaufman Astoria Studios in Queens. The funniest and most memorable scene is when Riggan (Michael Keaton) goes out for a smoke and locks himself out of the theater, and he has to dash around the block in his underwear through the crowds of Times Square to get back in through the front door. The scene was filmed at 2 a.m. in June to avoid having real bystanders in the shot. The production designer Kevin Thompson said, "We had crew pretending to be tourists taking video on their phones, plus a marching band to act as a protective wall around him. But a lot of people didn't recognize him. They thought he was just some crazy, wandering guy."

VANILLA SKY (2001)

Times Square

"My dreams are a cruel joke. They taunt me. Even in my dreams I'm an idiot . . . " —*David*

Vanilla Sky starts with an aerial shot over Manhattan that moves over buildings, Central Park, and finishes at the Dakota apartment building where the rich bachelor David (Tom Cruise) lives. David wakes up, grabs a list, his watch and driver's license, and drives a Porsche to Times Square, only to find it completely empty—not a single person is in the so-called "crossroads of the world," where approximately 300,000 people pass daily. Capturing this impossible scene was no CGI trick, however. It was filmed at the crack of dawn one Sunday morning in November, while the square was shut down for just three hours with help from New York's mayor's office and police department.

ENCHANTED (2007)

SCENES IN TIMES SQUARE

STAYING ALIVE (1983)
CROCODILE DUNDEE (1986)
NOW YOU SEE ME (2013)

87

TAXI DRIVER (1976)

47th Street and Eighth Avenue

"You talking to me?" —*Travis*

Suffering from insomnia, Travis (Robert De Niro), an ex-Marine and Vietnam War veteran, takes a job as a night-shift taxi driver. In the opening sequence, Travis goes to an adult movie theater on Eighth Avenue in the morning after work. The scene where he walks down the street with the Hollywood Theatre in the background became the famous publicity poster for the film. Though the corner has changed a lot since then, it still recalls the atmosphere (and smell) of Times Square in the '70s and '80s. Did you know that the famous scene where Travis is talking to himself in the mirror was completely ad-libbed by Robert De Niro? The screenplay details just said, "Travis looks in the mirror."

88

30 ROCK (2006–2013)

30 Rockefeller Plaza

"I want to go to there." —*Liz*

In the very first episode of *30 Rock*, Liz Lemon (Tina Fey), head writer of *The Girlie Show*, buys all the hot dogs a street vendor has just to thwart a man who tries to cut the line. She then walks through Rockefeller Plaza to her office and studio where she meets all the actors, writers, and executives who make her job difficult—and hilarious. The comedy show was based on Fey's experiences as head writer for *Saturday Night Live*, which is also filmed at 30 Rockefeller Plaza, a.k.a. 30 Rock. Did you know that the site of the Art Deco concrete jungle (Rockefeller Center) was the city's first public botanical garden, Elgin Botanic Garden, established in 1801 by David Hosack, the leading medical practitioner of his time?

MANHATTAN (1979)

Museum of Modern Art: 11 West 53rd Street

"Has anybody read that Nazis are gonna march in New Jersey?" —*Isaac*

One evening, at a Museum of Modern Art fundraising party, Isaac (Woody Allen) runs into Mary (Diane Keaton). They talk with some of her friends about the unlikely subjects of Nazis and orgasms. Then they leave the party together. As they walk along the city streets, they talk about Isaac quitting his job, his writing, her friends, and her past marriage. After picking up Mary's dog, the two take it for a walk, eventually sitting on a bench together as the sun rises over the Queensboro Bridge. It is said that the opening tune, George Gershwin's "Rhapsody in Blue" inspired the idea behind the film. Allen thought, 'This would be a beautiful thing to make a movie in black-and-white, you know, and make a romantic movie."

SEINFELD (1989–1998)

Soup Nazi (The Original Soup Man): 259-A West 55th Street

"No soup for you!" — *The Soup Nazi*

One of the most famous characters from Seinfeld history, the Soup Nazi first appeared in Season 7. Although the TV version of the shop is a studio set, the character is inspired by the real-life owner of The Original Soup Man (at 259-A West 55th Street). Jerry (Jerry Seinfeld), George (Jason Alexander), and Elaine (Julia Louis-Dreyfus) go to a new soup stand where the owner is known as the Soup Nazi for his short temper and nasty attitude. Because she annoys him, he refuses to sell Elaine her soup and she is banned from his store for one year. Elaine gets revenge by discovering his secret soup recipes. In real life, his actual customers referred to him as a terrorist, not a Nazi. "Next!"

MIDNIGHT COWBOY (1969)

56th Street and Sixth Avenue

"Hey! I'm walkin' here! I'm walkin' here!" —*Ratzo*

Ratzo (Dustin Hoffman) frantically explains the game of hustling and dealing with the "social register" gals, while Joe Buck (Jon Voight) listens. As they walk out into traffic, a yellow cab brakes within an inch of them. Ratzo screams the now famous line—"Hey! I'm walkin' here! I'm walkin' here!" as a cigarette flies out of his mouth and he slaps the cab's hood. The cab speeds off and he walks, unfazed, and says, "Actually that ain't a bad way to pick up insurance." Now known as an iconic New York scene, "I'm walkin' here!" is also known as one of the best film quotes ever. Some think it's an improvised line by Hoffman. But producer Jerome Hellman claims it was in the script. Film buffs like to believe the former.

LÉON: THE PROFESSIONAL (1994)

58th Street and Seventh Avenue

"Is life always this hard, or is it just when you're a kid?"
—Mathilda

Although Luc Besson wrote the script for *Léon* in only 30 days while waiting for the delayed shooting of *The Fifth Element*, this film is considered one of the greatest New York films. From interior scenes shot inside the Chelsea Hotel, to the street where hitman Léon (Jean Reno) and Mathilda (played by a 12-year-old Natalie Portman in her film debut) carry a forlorn houseplant as they move from one hotel to another, the film captures the gritty essence of 1990s New York—even though many interiors where shot on a Paris sound stage. Did you notice another scene where the characters are moving is filmed on Delancey Street?

HOME ALONE 2: LOST IN NEW YORK (1992)

The Plaza Hotel: 768 Fifth Avenue at 58th Street

Bellman: "You know, Herbert Hoover once stayed here on this floor." Kevin: "The vacuum guy?"

In the rush to get to O'Hare Airport on time for a holiday vacation, 10-year-old Kevin (Macaulay Culkin) mistakenly gets on a flight to New York City—and the rest of his family doesn't realize it until after they land in Miami. While his family panics, Kevin decides to enjoy Christmas vacation alone in New York. Using his Talkboy cassette recorder and his father's credit card, Kevin succeeds in checking into the luxurious Plaza Hotel. There he ends up spending $967 on room service, ordering chocolate cake, chocolate mousse, ice cream, and strawberry tarts...yum! The film was actually shot at the Plaza in a Central Park suite. And 12-year-old child actor Culkin was paid $4.5M for his role!

MIDTOWN WEST

81 **SLEEPLESS IN SEATTLE (1993)**

Empire State Building: 350 Fifth Avenue

Sam and Annie meet on the observation deck on Valentine's Day, thanks to Sam's 8-year-old son, Jonah.

82 **MIRACLE ON 34TH STREET (1947)**

Macy's: 151 West 34th Street

Kris Kringle rides in his sleigh in the Macy's Parade and waves to the cheering crowd.

83 **SEX AND THE CITY: THE MOVIE (2008)**

New York Public Library: 476 Fifth Avenue

Mr. Big's fear of marriage devastates Carrie, and she flees the huge wedding planned at the library.

84 **ONE FINE DAY (1996)**

Circle Line Sightseeing Cruise: Pier 83 at West 42nd Street

Maggie and Sammy miss their school field trip, arriving a few minutes too late at Pier 83 to board the Circle Line.

85 **BIRDMAN OR (THE UNEXPECTED VIRTUE OF IGNORANCE) (2014)** *St. James Theater: 246 West 44th Street*

Riggan, a former cinema superhero, hopes to reignite his career in an ambitious Broadway production.

86 **VANILLA SKY (2001)**

Times Square

David wakes up and drives his black Porsche to Times Square, only to find it completely empty.

87 **TAXI DRIVER (1976)**

47th Street and Eighth Avenue

Travis, a night-shift taxi driver, walks down a gritty, grimy, seedy Eighth Avenue in the morning after his shift ends.

88 **30 ROCK (2006–2013)**

30 Rockefeller Plaza

Liz, head writer of the sketch comedy, *The Girlie Show* works in the office and studio at 30 Rockefeller Plaza.

89 **MANHATTAN (1979)**

Museum of Modern Art: 11 West 53rd Street

Isaac runs into Mary at an Equal Rights Amendment fund-raising event at the museum.

90 **SEINFELD (1989–1998)**

Soup Nazi (The Original Soup Man): 259 West 55th Street

Jerry, George, and Elaine go to a new soup stand where the owner is referred to as The Soup Nazi.

94

95

96

98

99

MIDTOWN WEST

91 MIDNIGHT COWBOY (1969)
58th Street and Sixth Avenue

Ratso shouts "I'm walkin' here" to a passing cabbie who nearly hits him as he crosses the street.

92 LÉON: THE PROFESSIONAL (1994)
58th Street and Seventh Avenue

Léon and Mathilda carry a symbolic houseplant as they move from one hotel to another.

93 HOME ALONE 2: LOST IN NEW YORK (1992)
The Plaza Hotel: 768 Fifth Avenue

Kevin succeeds in checking in the hotel by himself by using his Talkboy tape recorder and his father's credit card.

94 HOW TO LOSE A GUY IN 10 DAYS (2003)
Madison Square Garden: 4 Pennsylvania Plaza

Without revealing their true intentions of why they are dating, Ben and Andie go to a New York Knicks game.

95 LETTERS TO JULIET (2010)
Bryant Park

Sophie receives an invitation from Claire and Lorenzo and decides to attend their wedding in Verona, Italy.

96 TOOTSIE (1982)
Theater Row on 42nd Street

Michael confesses, "I was a better man with you as a woman than I ever was with a woman as a man."

97 9½ WEEKS (1986)
The Algonquin Hotel: 59 West 44th Street

Wearing a man's suit, hat, and fake mustache, Elizabeth appears in the lobby bar in the hotel.

98 FAME (1980)
46th Street between Sixth and Seventh Avenues

Students of the School of Performing Arts stop traffic when their dancing spills out into the street.

99 SOMETHING'S GOTTA GIVE (2003)
Christie's: 20 Rockefeller Plaza

Harry is an aged music industry mogul with a fondness for younger women like Marin who works as an auctioneer.

100 THE DEVIL WEARS PRADA (2006)
1221 Avenue of the Americas

Andy struggles as a junior personal assistant to the impossible-to-please Miranda at the *Runway* magazine office.

MIDTOWN WEST

101 THE ADJUSTMENT BUREAU (2012)

Top of the Rock: 45 Rockefeller Plaza

David and Elise find themselves trapped and surrounded by the Bureau members on the observation deck.

102 ANNIE (1982)

Radio City Music Hall: 1260 Sixth Avenue

Annie, Grace and Daddy Warbucks have a private screening of a film at Radio City Music Hall.

103 NEW YEAR'S EVE (2011)

Stardust Diner: 1650 Broadway

After midnight on New Year's Eve, teenage Hailey meets her mother, Kim, at the diner before heading to an after-party.

104 SWEET SMELL OF SUCCESS (1957)

21 Club: 21 West 52nd Street

J. J. is dining at his customary booth with Senator Walker and company when Sidney joins them, against J. J.'s wishes.

105 HOME ALONE 2: LOST IN NEW YORK (1992)

Carnegie Hall: 881 Seventh Avenue

Kevin befriends the homeless pigeon lady in Central Park. They go to Carnegie Hall, where an orchestra is performing.

106 SEX AND THE CITY (1998–2004)

Da Marino Restaurant: 220 West 49th Street

Mr. Big serenades Carrie at the traditional Italian restaurant during their second try at a relationship.

107 SEX AND THE CITY (1998–2004)

Russian Samovar: 256 West 52nd Street

Carrie has a first date with the mysterious artist Aleksandr Petrovsky at the classic Russian restaurant.

108 SEX AND THE CITY (1998–2004)

Manolo Blahnik: 31 West 54th Street

Carrie admits that she has spent $40,000 on shoes—many of them Manolo Blahniks.

109 SEX AND THE CITY: THE MOVIE 2 (2010)

Ziegfeld Ballroom (Theatre): 141 West 54th Street

Miley Cyrus shares an air kiss with Samantha at a movie premiere, while both of them are wearing the same dress.

110 SEX AND THE CITY: THE MOVIE 2 (2010)

Bergdorf Goodman: 754 Fifth Avenue

The girls meet at the entrance of the store and buy wedding gifts for Anthony and Stanford.

REAR WINDOW (19

CHELSEA, UNION SQUARE & GREENWICH VILLAGE

THE AGE OF INNOCENCE (1993)

National Arts Club: 15 Gramercy Park South

"You gave me my first glimpse of a real life. Then you asked me to go on with the false one." —*Newland*

Adapted from the novel by Edith Wharton, the film depicts New York high society of the 1870s. After an opera at the Academy of Music (filmed at the Philadelphia Academy of Music), Newland Archer (Daniel Day-Lewis), May Welland (Winona Ryder) and the Countess Ellen Olenska (Michelle Pfeiffer) go to the Beauforts' for the opera ball. (Did you know that a man must change gloves each time he dances with a different woman at a ball?) The Beauforts' house (except the ball room) is the interior of the National Arts Club at Gramercy Park. The landmark building was built in the 1840s and purchased by Samuel Tilden, the 25th governor of New York in 1863. Wharton was born nearby at 14 West 23rd Street.

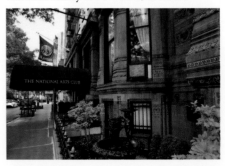

112

ACROSS THE UNIVERSE (2007)

Rooftop of the ABC Carpet Building: 19th Street and Broadway

"All you need is love."

Julie Taymor's fantasy musical film featuring 33 Beatles' classics tells the story of the love affair between Jude (Jim Sturgess), a Liverpool dockworker, and Lucy (Evan Rachel Wood), a girl from upper-crust East Coast suburbia, set amid the counterculture of 1960s politics, sex, drugs, and rock 'n' roll. The memorable last scene, which recalls the Beatles' famous rooftop concert, was shot on the roof of the ABC Carpet & Home building on Ladies' Mile; the street scene below was shot in TriBeCa at Desbrosses and Greenwich streets. The scene includes the iconic songs "Hey Jude," "Don't Let Me Down,"

"All You Need is Love," and the finale, "Lucy in the Sky with Diamonds."

113

THE HOURS (2002)

Meatpacking District: Hudson Street and 14th Street

"Mrs. Dalloway said she would buy the flowers herself."
—*Virginia Woolf and Laura Brown*

This acclaimed film explores the effect of Virginia Woolf's 1925 novel *Mrs. Dalloway* on three women of three different generations. One beautiful morning in the present day, editor Clarissa (Meryl Streep) visits the Meatpacking District loft of her longtime friend and former lover, the poet Richard (Ed Harris). She carries a bundle of flowers to cheer him up, and to convince him to attend his lifetime achievement award ceremony and party that evening. When she comes to pick him up for the ceremony in the afternoon, Richard, who is dying from AIDS, throws himself out of the window of his top-floor apartment, committing suicide.

AS GOOD AS IT GETS (1997)

Ardea: 31-33 West 12th Street

"You make me want to be a better man." —*Melvin*

A misanthropic, obsessive-compulsive novelist named Melvin (Jack Nicholson), and a gay artist, Simon (Greg Kinnear), live in the 1895-built, Beaux-Arts Ardea apartment building on 12th Street between Fifth and Sixth avenues. You can see the streets of Greenwich Village when Melvin walks Simon's dog, Verdell. Melvin is attracted to Carol (Helen Hunt), the only waitress who can tolerate him. What woman doesn't want to hear the compliment, "You make me want to be a better man," or "I might be the only person on the face of the earth that knows you're the greatest woman on earth." Both Nicholson and Hunt won Best Actor and Best Actress at the Academy Awards for their roles in this film.

FRIENDS (1994–2004)

The Friends Apartment: 90 Bedford Street at Grove Street

Rachel: "Okay. Should we get some coffee?"
Chandler: "Sure...Where?"

Rachel (Jennifer Aniston) moves into Monica's (Courtney Cox) apartment after running away from her wedding to her fiancé, Barry the dentist. Their sprawling two-bedroom apartment became the main stage of one of the most popular American sitcoms of all time. Who can forget the series finale when everyone leaves a copy of their keys on the counter on the way out to Central Perk for yet another cup of coffee and a new chapter in their lives? As a result of the show's huge success, the principal actors were paid $1 million in the final two seasons, from $22,500 per episode in the first season, making Aniston, Cox, and Kudrow the highest-paid TV actresses of all time.

AUGUST RUSH (2007)

Washington Square Park

"The music is all around us. All you have to do is listen."
—*August Rush*

On a rooftop terrace looking down on Washington Square Park, cellist Lyla (Keri Russell) and guitarist Louis (Jonathan Rhys Meyers) share an enchanted night together under a full moon, then go their separate ways. They have a son together, whom Louis doesn't know about and whom Lyla believes died in an accident. Eleven years later, the boy, Evan (Freddie Highmore), runs away from the orphanage where he was raised to New York City, in hopes of discovering his roots. A child prodigy, he starts playing guitar as a street performer in the same park where his musician parents first met. It's music that finally brings them back together.

SCENES IN WASHINGTON SQUARE PARK

SEX AND THE CITY (1998-2004)

Carrie's Apartment: 66 Perry Street

"People make mistakes." —*Carrie*

In season three, Carrie's love interest Mr. Big (Chris Noth) marries Natasha (Bridget Moynahan), while Carrie (Sarah Jessica Parker) meets a cute furniture designer, Aidan (John Corbett). Carrie throws out her cigarettes and slaps on the patch for Aiden, and then suffers a crisis when she realizes that their relationship is drama-free. Married Mr. Big still pursues Carrie, and the love triangle between Carrie, Aidan and Mr. Big begins. Did you notice that Bridget Moynahan (as Natasha/Halley) and John Corbit (as Aidan/Lars) play the characters who have claims on the main characters in the show, and in Serendipity (2001) Chris Noth

has a cameo during Jonathan and Halley's engagement party?

CHELSEA, UNION SQUARE & GREENWICH VILLAGE

111 THE AGE OF INNOCENCE (1993)

The Beaufort's House: The National Arts Club

After the opera, Mrs. Beaufort always hosts an annual ball at her grand home, which is one of the few with a ballroom.

112 ACROSS THE UNIVERSE (2007)

Rooftop of the ABC Carpet Building: 888 Broadway

Sadie, Jojo, and Jude play "Don't Let Me Down" and "All You Need is Love" on the rooftop.

113 THE HOURS (2002)

Hudson Street and 14th Street

Clarissa, carrying a bunch of flowers, visits Richard's loft in the Meatpacking District.

114 AS GOOD AS IT GETS (1997)

Ardea: 31–33 West 12th Street

Melvin and Simon live in the 1895 Beaux-Arts apartment building on West 12th Street.

115 FRIENDS (1994-2004)

The Friends Apartment: 90 Bedford Street

Monica's purple-walled apartment that she sublets from her grandmother is the main stage of the show.

116 AUGUST RUSH (2007)

Washington Square Park

August meets Louis at the park and they play guitar together without knowing they are blood relatives.

117 SEX AND THE CITY (1998–2004)

Carrie's Apartment: 66 Perry Street

The steps where Carrie often sat are real, although the fictional location is "245 East 73rd Street."

118 SPIDER-MAN (2002)

The Daily Bugle: Flatiron Building: 175 Fifth Avenue

After he graduates from high school, Peter works as a freelance photographer for the newspaper, the *Daily Bugle*.

119 SID AND NANCY (1986)

Hotel Chelsea: 222 West 23rd Street

Sid and Nancy fight in a drug-induced haze and he later stabs her in the hotel room after she begs him to kill her.

120 MEN IN BLACK II (2002)

Empire Dinner: 210 Tenth Avenue

Agent J and Tee eat pie at the diner. Tee starts blubbering because he knows that Jay is going to neutralize him.

CHELSEA, UNION SQUARE & GREENWICH VILLAGE

121 SERENDIPITY (2001)

Chelsea Pier 59: West 18th Street and Eleventh Avenue

Sara sees the flier about Chelsea Piers and feels the need to go there immediately, thinking that's where Jonathan might be.

122 ALMOST FAMOUS (2000)

Gramercy Park Hotel: 2 Lexington Avenue

Driving over the Queensboro Bridge, Stillwater and William get to Manhattan and check into the rock-star haven hotel.

123 MAN ON A LEDGE (2012)

Old Town Bar: 45 East 18th Street

Nick meets Joey, Angie, and Lydia, and introduces Lydia to the hotel concierge, who is Nick's father.

124 PRIME (2005)

Village Cinema: 22 East 12th Street

While standing in line with her friends, Rafi, recently divorced, is introduced to a younger man, David.

125 I AM LEGEND (2007)

Neville's Townhouse: 11 Washington Square

Neville lives in a heavily fortified townhouse with a laboratory in the basement.

126 MO' BETTER BLUES (1990)

Cherry Lane Theater: 38 Commerce Street

Bleek performs on the trumpet at a busy nightclub, Beneath the Underdog with his jazz band, The Bleek Quintet.

127 SPIDER-MAN 2 (2004)

Joe's Pizza: 7 Carmine Street

When he makes a late delivery, Parker is sacked from his job delivering pizzas for Joe's Pizza in Greenwich Village.

128 SLEEPERS (1996)

Minetta Tavern: 113 MacDougal Street

Shakes and his old buddies celebrate at the bar after Michael, now assistant district attorney, blows the case against them.

129 SERPICO (1973)

Serpico's Apartment: 5-7 Minetta Street

Serpico leaves Brooklyn, crossing the Williamsburg Bridge to start a new life at the apartment in Greenwich Village.

130 NEXT STOP, GREENWICH VILLAGE (1976)

Caffe Reggio: 119 MacDougal Street

Larry, Sarah and his friends regularly gather at the Village's oldest coffee house, first opened in 1927.

CHELSEA, UNION SQUARE & GREENWICH VILLAGE

131 SEX AND THE CITY (1998–2004)
Church of the Transfiguration: 1 East 29th Street
The "Little Church Around the Corner" is where Samantha meets a hot priest, "the Friar."

132 SEX AND THE CITY (1998–2004)
Eleven Madison Park: 11 Madison Avenue
Mr. Big meets Carrie at the upscale restaurant to tell her that he is engaged to another woman.

133 SEX AND THE CITY (1998–2004)
Pete's Tavern: 129 East 18th Street
Miranda proposes to Steve over $3 beers at Pete's Tavern, an old-time NYC favorite, open since 1864.

134 SEX AND THE CITY (1998–2004)
City Bakery: 3 West 18th Street
Carrie and Samantha discuss "the face girl" over lunch and Carrie proclaims "the best brownies in New York."

135 SEX AND THE CITY: THE MOVIE (2008)
Buddakan: 75 Ninth Avenue
Carrie and Big's rehearsal dinner is held at this lavish Asian restaurant in the Meatpacking District.

136 SEX AND THE CITY: THE MOVIE (2008)
Diane von Furstenberg: 874 Washington Street
As Carrie browses, she talks on her cell phone with Samantha about her and Big's decision to get married.

137 SEX AND THE CITY (1998–2004)
Magnolia Bakery: 401 Bleecker Street
In an attempt to quit smoking for her new man Aidan, Carrie turns to cake, and joins Miranda for cupcakes.

138 SEX AND THE CITY (1998–2004)
The Pleasure Chest: 156 Seventh Avenue South
The girls go shopping for their own toys at this high-end adult store, and even Charlotte develops a "Rabbit" habit.

139 SEX AND THE CITY (1998–2004)
Il Cantinori: 32 East 10th Street
Carrie celebrates her 35th birthday all by herself at this Tuscan restaurant because her friends got the address wrong.

140 SEX AND THE CITY (1998–2004)
Jefferson Market Garden
Miranda and Steve's wedding ceremony takes place in a community garden, the former site of a women's prison.

EAST VILLAGE, LOWER EAST SIDE & NOLITA

THE FRENCH CONNECTION (19

GREAT EXPECTATIONS (1998)

Tompkins Square Park

"It's my heart, and it's broken." —*Finn*

This modernized version of Charles Dickens's novel moves the setting from 1810–20s London to 1990s New York. Finn Bell, a 10-year-old boy living in a Florida fishing village, falls in love with the beautiful Estella, a niece of the rich Mrs. Dinsmoor, who gave him a surprise kiss while drinking water from a fountain at her mansion. Seven years later, Finn (Ethan Hawke) makes the move to New York and begins his new life, struggling to become a successful artist. With just 10 weeks to complete the necessary paintings for his first gallery show, Finn begins drawing at the East Village's Tompkins Square Park, where he again encounters Estella (Gwyneth Paltrow), once again re-creating the water-fountain kiss of their childhood.

THE GODFATHER PART II (1974)

6th Street between Avenues A & B

"Keep your friends close, but your enemies closer."
—*Michael Corleone*

In 1917, Vito Corleone (Robert De Niro) lives in a tenement with his family and is an honest grocery store clerk. Three years later he shoots and kills Don Fanucci (Gastone Moschin) during the Feast of San Rocco, which begins his transformation into the respected and feared Don Corleone. It took six months to transform East 6th Street into the Little Italy of 1917—including the installation of new storefronts and signs, re-painting buildings, and changing lampposts. The grocery store where Vito works and where Don Fanucci lives is set at 523 and 538 East 6th Street. Francis Ford Coppola originally did not want to direct Part II because of a tense relationship with Paramount, and he recommended Martin Scorsese instead.

WHEN HARRY MET SALLY... (1989)

Katz's Delicatessen: 205 East Houston Street

"I'll have what she's having." —*a woman nearby*

One of the most unforgettable scenes in movie history is Sally's (Meg Ryan) dramatic performance at Katz's Delicatessen. Over pastrami sandwiches, Sally tries to convince her longtime friend Harry (Billy Crystal) that men can't tell when women "fake it." Her logic? "It's just that all men are sure it never happened to them and all women at one time or other have done it so you do the math." Then she expressively proves her point as customers watch. When she finishes, a woman at a nearby table (played by director Rob Reiner's mother) places her order: "I'll have what she's having." The table where the scene was filmed has a plaque on it that reads, "Where Harry met Sally...hope you have what she had!—Enjoy!"

144

ETERNAL SUNSHINE OF THE SPOTLESS MIND (2004) *Orchard Street and Rivington Street*

"Leave you at the flea market with this stupid costume jewelry!" —*Clementine*

Joel (Jim Carrey) and Clementine (Kate Winslet) have been in a turbulent relationship for two years. One day while together at a flea market on Orchard Street on the Lower East Side, they get into an argument about having a baby. After a nasty breakup each decides to have the other erased from their memories, only to meet again unknowingly at a diner in Montauk. They then rekindle their relationship on the Long Island Railroad, in scenes shot on a real, moving train. Did you notice that Clementine's hair color changes, from blue, to orange, red, green, and brown, which helps the viewer keep track of where her relationship with Joel corresponds to the plot?

P.S. I LOVE YOU (2007)

Holly and Gerry's Apartment: 254 Broome Street

"Every morning I still wake up and the first thing I want to do is to see your face." —*Gerry*

As the film opens, Holly (Hilary Swank) and Gerry (Gerard Butler) appear from the East Broadway subway station and argue over an incident at dinner as they walk back to their apartment on the Lower East Side. Gerry dies suddenly of a brain tumor, but not before arranging messages ending with "P.S. I love you" to be delivered to Holly after his death. The letters send her on a journey to Ireland, as she slowly regains the confidence to love again. Despite the fact that Holly and Gerry are Irish and live in Ireland in the original novel by Cecelia Ahern, in the film only Gerry is Irish and they live in New York, yet all of Gerry's letters are virtually unchanged.

THE GODFATHER PART III (1990)

Elizabeth Street between Prince and East Houston Streets

"Finance is a gun. Politics is knowing when to pull the trigger." —*Don Lucchesi*

Much of The Godfather Trilogy takes place in the historic Little Italy neighborhood, on the streets around Saint Patrick's Old Cathedral. It is here, on Elizabeth Street, that Vincent Mancini (Andy Garcia) kills enemy mob boss Zasa, while disguised as a policeman. Though the street is now part of trendy NoLita (short for north of Little Italy) and lined with cafés and boutiques, you can still feel the atmosphere from the film with a short walk to the center of Little Italy: Mulberry Street between Broome and Grand streets. Visit in September to experience the annual feast of San Gennaro, when vendors line the street.

THE GODFATHER (1972)

Genco Pura Olive Oil Co.: 128 Mott Street

"I'm gonna make him an offer he can't refuse."
—*Don Corleone*

Don Corleone (Marlon Brando) is gunned down in front of his office at Genco Olive Oil. He is shot several times in the back but survives. Fredo Corleone (John Cazale), Michael's (Al Pacino) older brother, was in charge of protecting his father when the Don's bodyguard called in sick. But Fredo proves inept; he fumbles with his gun and doesn't shoot back. The scene was shot at 128 Mott Street in Chinatown. The first floor of the gigantic building is now a Chinese grocery store and Mott Street is a busy shopping area. Little Italy is a block over, and continues along Mulberry Street. Did you notice that Brando wore a mouthpiece made by a dentist to make his cheeks puff out like a bulldog for his role?

EAST VILLAGE, LOWER EAST SIDE & NOLITA

141 **GREAT EXPECTATIONS (1998)**

Tompkins Square Park

Finn encounters Estella again by recreating the
water-fountain kiss of their childhood.

142 **THE GODFATHER PART II (1974)**

6th Street between Avenues A and B

Young Vito Corleone murders Don Fanucci during the feast
of San Rocco in Little Italy.

143 **WHEN HARRY MET SALLY… (1989)**

Katz's Delicatessen: 205 East Houston Street

Sally famously fakes an orgasm at the deli to prove her point
that a man can't tell the difference as other customers watch.

144 **ETERNAL SUNSHINE OF THE SPOTLESS
MIND (2004)** *Orchard Street and Rivington Street*

Walking through the flea market, Clementine and Joel get
into an argument about having a baby.

145 **P.S. I LOVE YOU (2007)**

Holly and Gerry's Apartment: 254 Broome Street

Holly and Gerry walk back to their apartment while arguing
over an incident at dinner.

146 **THE GODFATHER PART III (1990)**

Elizabeth Street between Prince and East Houston Streets

Vincent, disguised as a mounted policeman, kills his enemy,
the mafia boss Zasa, during a procession in Little Italy.

147 **THE GODFATHER (1972)**

Genco Pura Olive Oil Co.: 128 Mott Street

Godfather Vito Corleone is shot on the street in front of
Genco Co. by Sollozzo's men and lands in the hospital.

148 **TAXI DRIVER (1976)**

Iris' Brothel: 226 East 13th Street

To save Iris, Travis shoots Sport, her pimp, and her
customers, then tries to shoot himself but runs out of bullets.

149 **NICK AND NORAH'S INFINITE PLAYLIST
(2008)** *Veselka: 144 Second Avenue*

Nick calls Norah, apologizing for leaving, and she meets him
again at the 24-hour Ukrainian diner.

150 **TWO WEEKS NOTICE (2002)**

St. Marks Church-in-the-Bowery: 131 East 10th Street

Lucy's cell phone rings while she is at her friend's wedding,
and she leaves to help George select a suit for an event.

ROOMS

148

152

156

158

EAST VILLAGE, LOWER EAST SIDE & NOLITA

151 ONCE UPON A TIME IN AMERICA (1984)

McSorley's Old Ale House: 15 East 7th Street

Young gang members debate whether to take the dollar the bartender offers them to burn a newsstand or roll the drunk.

152 CROCODILE DUNDEE (1986)

Vazaks Horseshoe Bar: 108 Avenue B

A taxi driver takes Mick to this favorite bar in Alphabet City to introduce him to New York "wildlife."

153 FRIENDS WITH BENEFITS (2011)

Café Habana: 17 Prince Street

Jamie and Dylan open up to each other while having lunch revealing they're both regarded as "emotionally unavailable."

154 NICK AND NORAH'S INFINITE PLAYLIST (2008) *Arlene's Grocery: 95 Stanton Street*

Nora comes to see Nick's band The Jerk-Offs perform at the club on Manhattan's Lower East Side.

155 ACROSS THE UNIVERSE (2007)

Rivington Street and Clinton Street

Jojo arrives in the 1960s East Village after his younger brother is killed in the Detroit riots.

156 THE NAKED CITY (1948)

Williamsburg Bridge: Delancey Street and the East River

Garzah runs up the esplanade and tries to escape by climbing up a tower. He is shot by police and falls to his death.

157 MEAN STREETS (1973)

Old St. Patrick's Cathedral: 264 Mulberry Street

Torn between work for his uncle and his Catholic beliefs, Charlie sacrifices himself on Johnny's behalf.

158 DONNIE BRASCO (1997)

Mulberry Street Bar: 176 Mulberry Street

Donnie, posing as a jewel thief, earns Lefty's trust by convincing him that a diamond dealer is selling him a fake.

159 SEX AND THE CITY (1998–2004)

St. Mark's Comics: 11 St. Marks Place

Carrie meets mama's boy Wade, a 30-something still living with his parents, who spends his money on pot.

160 SEX AND THE CITY (1998–2004)

Joe's Pub: 425 Lafayette Street

Carrie meets Ray the bass-player while out with Mr. Big at this Noho nightclub.

SOHO &
TRIBECA

GHOST

GHOST (1990)

Sam and Molly's Loft: 102 Prince Street

"It's amazing, Molly. The love inside, you take it with you."
—*Sam*

Wall Street banker Sam (Patrick Swayze) and his artist girlfriend Molly (Demi Moore) move into a cast-iron building on Prince Street in SoHo. Unable to sleep the night after they move, Molly begins casting pots at 2 a.m. Sam wakes up and grabs Molly from behind, clay sliding between their fingers as the pottery wheel spins, and the Righteous Brothers' 1965 song "Unchained Melody" rises in the background. Their happiness is short-lived, however, as Sam is murdered soon after, and he haunts his love in order to uncover the truth behind his death. Soho's huge loft spaces and low rent was a mecca for artists and art galleries until the 90s, after which it was transformed into the high-end fashionable shopping area it is today.

UNFAITHFUL (2002)

Paul's Loft: 70 Mercer Street

"There is no such thing as a mistake. There are things you do, and things you don't do." —*Paul*

Unfaithful was adapted from the 1969 French film *La Femme infidèle* by Claude Chabrol. During a trip to Manhattan to shop for her son's birthday party, Connie (Diane Lane), is caught in a heavy windstorm in SoHo. She collides with a young man, Paul (Olivier Martinez), and falls and scrapes her knee. Paul invites her to his apartment for a bandage, which leads to their fatal affair. The opening windstorm sequence was shot at the corner of Mercer and Broome streets, and Paul's loft is inside 70 Mercer Street. Nearby Café Noir (32 Grand Street), where they passionately make love in the bathroom while Connie's friends wait for her at the table, is gone, although the bathroom scene was filmed on a sound stage.

GHOSTBUSTERS (1984)

Hook & Ladder Company 8: 14 North Moore Street

"We came. We saw. We kicked its ass." —*Dr. Peter Venkman*

Fired from their jobs researching the paranormal at Columbia University, oddball scientists Peter (Bill Murray), Raymond (Dan Aykroyd), and Egon (Harold Ramis) set up a supernatural extermination service in a retired firehouse. While they face some skeptics at first, before long the Ghostbusters are the most in-demand service in town. Since the real-life Hook & Ladder Company 8 is an active firehouse, interior scenes were filmed at Fire Station No. 23 in downtown Los Angeles. The New York firehouse is still in use, and if you pass by you can still see the sign from the film hanging up inside, as well as a Ghostbusters badge painted on the sidewalk.

SOHO & TRIBECA

161 GHOST (1990)

Sam and Molly's Loft: 102 Prince Street

Sam and Molly move into a loft in a cast-iron building in SoHo, which was the actual home of an artist/sculptor.

162 UNFAITHFUL (2002)

Paul's Loft: 70 Mercer Street

After Connie collides with Paul and she falls and scrapes her knee, Paul invites her to his loft for a bandage.

163 GHOSTBUSTERS (1984)

Hook & Ladder Company 8: 14 North Moore Street

Walter releases hundreds of captured ghosts into the city from the basement of Ghostbusters' headquarters.

164 PRIME (2005)

Dean & DeLuca: 560 Broadway

Rafi and David bump into each other at the SoHo gourmet store and they start seeing each other again.

165 HITCH (2005)

Greene Street and Spring Street

Hitch jumps on Sara's car in hopes of getting back with her. "There's only one person that makes me feel like I can fly. . ."

166 9 1/2 WEEKS (1986)

Elizabeth's Gallery: 101 Spring Street

Elizabeth, a gallery employee, has a brief but steamy, erotic affair with John, a Wall Street broker.

167 TWO WEEKS NOTICE (2002)

Roxy Hotel: 2 Sixth Avenue

Lucy finds George and June playing strip chess, he in boxers, she in a bra and slip, at his hotel residence in TriBeCa.

168 DEFINITELY, MAYBE (2008)

The Odeon: 145 West Broadway

Summer writes an offensive article about a client of Will's causing Will to lose his business.

169 SEX AND THE CITY (1998-2004)

Louis K. Meisel Gallery: 141 Prince Street

Charlotte has a coveted job at the gallery, but quits when she decides to marry Trey and focus on getting pregnant.

170 SEX AND THE CITY (1998-2004)

Onieals: 174 Grand Street

The bar is the setting for Scout, the bar Steve names after his dog and runs with a silent partner, Aidan.

BASQUIAT (1996)
SEX AND THE CITY (1998-2004)

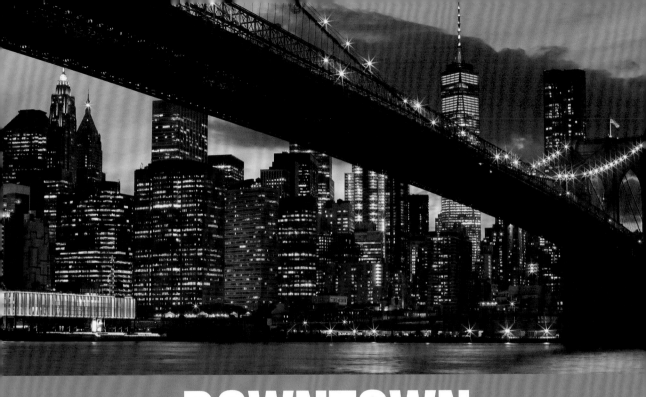

DOWNTOWN
& DUMBO

ON THE TOWN (1949)

GANGS OF NEW YORK (2002)

Five Points: Paradise Square

"WOOPSY DAISY!" —Bill *"The Butcher"*

The notoriously violent Five Points covered five blocks centered on the intersection of Cross Street, Anthony Street (today's Worth), and Orange Street (today's Baxter), and the current southwest corner of Columbus Park in Chinatown. Paradise Square, site of scenes including the fight between Amsterdam Vallon (Leonardo DiCaprio) and Bill "The Butcher" Cutting (Daniel Day-Lewis), is adjacent, now occupied by the New York State Supreme Court building. Where was the movie filmed? Martin Scorsese had the 19th-century Five Points recreated in Cinecittà Studios in Rome. New York history buffs love seeing Boss Tweed, Bill "The Butcher," the Old Brewery, the draft riots of 1863 and the Bandit's Roost. Can you picture Paradise Square, standing on the actual site?

KATE & LEOPOLD (2001)

Brooklyn Bridge

"Good Lord, it still stands. The world has changed all around it, but Roebling's erection still stands!" —*Leopold*

The film begins with views of the Brooklyn Bridge under construction. The Brooklyn Bridge, completed in 1883, was the longest suspension bridge in the world, thanks to the efforts of the Roebling family. Leopold (Hugh Jackman), a duke who travels through time from 1876 New York to the 21st century, falls in love with Kate (Meg Ryan), a career woman in modern New York. When she discovers her time-traveling beau's secret, Kate decides to chase Leopold through a time window that opens at the Brooklyn Bridge. Did you know P.T. Barnum, who Jackman plays in *The Greatest Showman* (2017) marched 21 elephants over the bridge to test its durability in 1884?

MO' BETTER BLUES (1990)

I AM LEGEND (2007)

South Street Seaport

> **"I will be at the South Street Seaport every day at midday, when the sun is highest in the sky." —Robert**

In 2012, virologist Robert Neville (Will Smith) is the last healthy human living in New York after a devastating outbreak. When he loses his dog, he takes revenge on infected vampiric humans. When he is nearly killed at the South Street Seaport, a pair of immune humans from Maryland, Anna (Alice Braga) and Ethan (Charlie Tahan) save his life, and encourage him to continue with them to a survivor's colony in Vermont. The dramatic flashback scene of the evacuation of New York was filmed over six consecutive nights in January on the Brooklyn Bridge with 1,000 extras and various military vehicles and aircraft at the cost of $5 million—believed to be the most expensive shoot in New York film history.

13 GOING ON 30 (2004)

Brooklyn Bridge Park: Empire–Fulton Ferry

"You know what I wish I had right now?" "No, what?" "Razzles." —*Jenna and Matt*

After a prank is played on her at her 13th birthday party, Jenna (Jennifer Garner) wakes up to discover she is a successful fashion magazine editor with a Fifth Avenue apartment. She tracks down her one-time best friend Matt (Mark Ruffalo), a struggling photographer, who she mistakenly blamed for the prank 17 years earlier, and together they work on a magazine project. One night they buy Razzles candy, Jenna's favorite, and take a walk in the park after checking photos for the project. With a beautiful nighttime view of Manhattan and the Brooklyn Bridge at Empire-Fulton Park they become closer again and kiss.

175

ONCE UPON A TIME IN AMERICA (1984)

Washington and Water Streets, Brooklyn

"When you've been betrayed by a friend, you hit back. Do it." —*Secretary Bailey*

Noodles, Max, Patsy, Cockeye, and Little Dominic are a gang of Jewish kids living on the Lower East Side in the 1920s. They make their first big score, by hiding a shipment of bootlegged alcohol. After keeping the money in a locker at the train station they are attacked by their former boss Bugsy, and Dominic is shot to death on the street near the Manhattan Bridge—their happy moment suddenly turning to tragedy. The original cut by director Sergio Leone was 3 hours and 49 minutes long; the film was cut to 2 hours and 19 minutes for the theatrical release in 1984. It was restored to its original length on video and DVD.

THE DARK KNIGHT RISES (2012)

Wall Street

Catwoman: "You don't owe these people any more. You've given them everything." Batman: "Not everything. Not yet."

With *The Dark Night Rises*, Christopher Nolan completed the Trilogy that he began with *Batman Begins* (2005) and *The Dark Knight* (2008). The scene where Bane's (Tom Hardy) team robs the Gotham City Stock Exchange was filmed at the JP Morgan Building at 23 Wall Street, directly across from the New York Stock Exchange. The clash between Gotham City Police, led by Batman (Christian Bain) and escaped inmates from Arkham Asylum, was filmed with hundreds of extras duking it out at a smoke-filled intersection of Wall Street and William Street. The shooting was done on a weekend in October, 2011, and notices billed the production as "Magnus Rex" in a feeble effort to keep the shooting a secret.

INSIDE MAN (2006)

20 Exchange Place

"My friends and I are making a very large withdrawal from this bank. Anybody gets in our way, gets a bullet in the brain." —*Dalton*

Dalton (Clive Owen) and his gang have come up with a foolproof plan to rob a bank. Their target? Manhattan Trust Bank near Wall Street. They lock the doors and take hostages and then finally request two buses and an airplane to escape. Detective Keith Frazier (Denzel Washington) is assigned to negotiate with Dalton, but the case is more complicated than it seems. The Hanover Street entrance of the building at 20 Exchange Place was used as a main entrance for the bank. "It looked like the perfect bank robbery. But you can't judge a crime by its cover."

CROCODI

SCENES AT DOWNTOWN OFFICE BUILDINGS

SABRINA (1954)
THE DEVIL'S ADVOCAT
THE APARTMENT (1960

DESPERATELY SEEKING SUSAN (1986)

The Battery

"Desperately Seeking Susan, Keep the faith, Tuesday 10 a.m. Battery Park Gangway 1." —*Jim*

Roberta (Rosanna Arquette), a bored suburban housewife from New Jersey, is fascinated by a stranger named Susan(Madonna) after reading messages of love in the personal ads of a New York paper. Following an ad from the paper, Roberta goes to The Battery (Battery Park) to witness the rendezvous. Roberta then tries to meet Susan at the park but gets hit on the head. When she wakes up with amnesia, she is mistaken for Susan, and the fun begins. The film was released just as Madonna became popular, and includes her hit "Into the Groove," played during the Danceteria scene. Danceteria, at 30 West 21st Street, has since turned into condos. When Madonna was a hat-check girl there, she convinced the DJ to play her demo tape.

WORKING GIRL (1988)

Staten Island Ferry

"Hey, Cyn. Guess where I am." —*Tess* from her new job in her private office

As the inspirational Oscar-winning song, "Let the River Run" sung by Carly Simon plays, the film opens with a panorama of the Statue of Liberty. The camera then focuses on the Staten Island Ferry and Tess (Melanie Griffith) on her way to her menial office job in Manhattan. The ferry, a free 25-minute ride, connects Whitehall Terminal in Lower Manhattan and St. George Terminal in Staten Island, 365 days a year. Later, we see a sad Tess back on the ferry on her way home. Remember the scene when Tess "borrows" her boss's designer dress, drinks tequila at an office party and ends up in bed with Jack Trainer (Harrison Ford)? During the filming, Griffith's only Oscar nominated performance, she was actually battling alcohol and cocaine addiction.

GHOSTBUSTERS II (1989)

Statue of Liberty

"Whether she's naked under that toga. She *is* French. You know that." —*Dr. Peter Venkman*

Five years after the events of the first film, Ghostbusters (Bill Murray, Dan Aykroyd, Harold Ramis, and Ernie Hudson) use a slime-coated Statue of Liberty to enter the Manhattan Museum of Art. As they play the song "Higher and Higher," they pilot the statue through New York Harbor and the streets to cheering crowds. The statue's torch breaks the museum's ceiling to attack Vigo. The museum is actually The National Museum of the American Indian in the Alexander Hamilton U.S. Customs House at 1 Bowling Green. However, since Lady Liberty is 111 feet tall from heel to crown, and nowhere between Liberty Island and Manhattan is over 60 feet deep, she should only be about waist deep.

DOWNTOWN & DUMBO

171 GANGS OF NEW YORK (2002)

Paradise Square

Paradise Square is the site of scenes including the fight between Amsterdam Vallon and Bill "The Butcher" Cutting.

172 KATE & LEOPOLD (2001)

Brooklyn Bridge

Leopold follows Stuart and they fall into a temporal portal between centuries.

173 I AM LEGEND (2007)

South Street Seaport

After Sam is attacked by infected dogs, Neville seeks revenge against the Darkseekers.

174 13 GOING ON 30 (2004)

Empire–Fulton Ferry Park, Brooklyn

After checking photos for a magazine story, Jenna and Matt take a nighttime walk in the park and end up kissing.

175 ONCE UPON A TIME IN AMERICA (1984)

Washington Street and Water Street, Brooklyn

Little Dominic is shot to death by Bugsy on the street along the Brooklyn waterfront near the Manhattan Bridge.

176 THE DARK KNIGHT RISES (2012)

Wall Street

Batman frees the trapped Gotham City Police and they clash with Bane's army on Wall Street.

177 INSIDE MAN (2006)

Manhattan Trust Bank: 20 Exchange Place

Dalton and his company rob Manhattan Trust Bank and take the patrons and employees as hostages.

178 DESPERATELY SEEKING SUSAN (1985)

Battery Park

Curious to see the outcome of an ad in a tabloid, Roberta goes to Battery Park to spy on Susan's rendezvous.

179 WORKING GIRL (1988)

Staten Island Ferry

Tess commutes to her office at an investment bank on Wall Street on the Staten Island Ferry.

180 GHOSTBUSTERS II (1989)

Statue of Liberty

The Ghostbusters use positively-charged mood slime to animate the Statue of Liberty and pilot it to the museum.

DOWNTOWN & DUMBO

181 ANGER MANAGEMENT (2003)

New York County Courthouse: 60 Centre Street

Dave is found guilty of assault and sentenced to anger-management therapy.

182 THE WOLF OF WALL STREET (2013)

North Cove Marina: 250 Vesey Street

Patrick, an FBI agent, comes to see Jordan on his yacht anchored in the marina near Ground Zero.

183 ANNIE HALL (1977)

Pier 16

Alvy and Annie spend a romantic night together. "Love is too weak a word for what I feel - I luuurve you . . . "

184 DIE HARD WITH A VENGEANCE (1995)

Federal Reserve Bank: 33 Liberty Street

Simon steals $140 billion in gold bullion from the Federal Reserve Bank while a subway explosion distracts the police.

185 NATIONAL TREASURE (2004)

Trinity Church: 75 Broadway

Beneath the church Ben, Riley, Abigail, and Patrick finally find the vast treasure trove.

186 KATE & LEOPOLD (2001)

Leopold's House: 1 Hanover Square

Leopold finds his mother's ring in his hidden drawer at his still-existing house after 125 years.

187 HOW TO LOSE A GUY IN 10 DAYS (2003)

Alexander Hamilton Custom House

At the company ball Andie and Ben sing a poor version of "You're So Vain" to try to humiliate each other.

188 MEN IN BLACK (1997)

M.I.B. Headquarters: 504 Battery Place

Edwards passes the test and becomes Agent J and with Agent K he often reports back to the Men in Black Headquarters.

189 HITCH (2005)

Ellis Island

Hitch shows Sara her great-great grandfather's entry in a ledger on Ellis Island, but she is not happy to be reminded.

190 SEX AND THE CITY (1998−2004)

Century 21: 22 Cortlandt Street

Carrie enjoys bargain hunting at the Financial District location while she is on jury duty at the courthouse nearby.

SERPICO (1

BROOKLYN

191

THE FRENCH CONNECTION (1971)

62nd Street Station

"Did you ever pick your feet in Poughkeepsie?"
—*Jimmy "Popeye" Doyle*

The film, based on the 1969 book by Robin Moore, is about a 1961 drug bust by New York cops, Jimmy "Popeye" Doyle (Gene Hackman) and Buddy "Cloudy" Russo (Roy Scheider). The film won five Oscars and set the standard for police-themed dramas. The famous car chase where Popeye takes over a civilian's car and chases a hitman on a subway train was filmed beneath the Stillwell Avenue tracks in Brooklyn over five weeks, with police clearing five blocks at a time. Popeye shoots the hitman at the 62nd Street Station, at New Utrecht Avenue. Ironically, the two-car crash at Stillwell Avenue and 86th Street was unplanned. A man on his way to work was unaware that a car chase was being filmed. The producers paid his repair bill.

192

SATURDAY NIGHT FEVER (1977)

86th Street, Bensonhurst

"Well I mean, I could dance with you, but you're not my dream girl or nothing like that..." —*Tony*

Saturday Night Fever opens with an aerial shot from the Brooklyn Bridge to the neighborhood of Bay Ridge in Brooklyn, emphasizing its distance from Manhattan. Then 18-year-old Brooklyn native Tony Manero (John Travolta) appears, strutting down 86th Street to the Bee Gees' song, "Stayin' Alive." He buys two slices of pizza at Lenny's Pizza and keeps on walking. The film was based on a 1976 story from *New York* magazine, though the author later admitted it was fabricated. The huge commercial success of this film significantly helped to popularize disco music around the world and, of course, John Travolta too.

UPTOWN GIRLS (2003)

Coney Island, Brooklyn

"We are going to sit in giant teacups and spin round and round in circles until we puke." —*Molly*

The spoiled daughter of a dead rock star, Molly (Brittany Murphy), and the 8-year-old daughter of a busy executive, Ray (Dakota Fanning), both feel painfully alone in the world. When she loses her money, Molly is forced to take a job as Ray's babysitter, and though the carefree nanny and serious child don't get along at first, the two begin to bond. When Ray's comatose father dies, Molly finds the missing girl at the Coney Island boardwalk, riding a giant teacup. After Ray throws up, she slaps Molly and punches her, as if trying to let all her anger out. Molly hugs her and each discovers a true friend in the other.

SCENES AT CONEY ISLAND

WONDER WHEEL (2017)
THE WARRIORS (1979)
REQUIEM FOR A DREAM (2000)

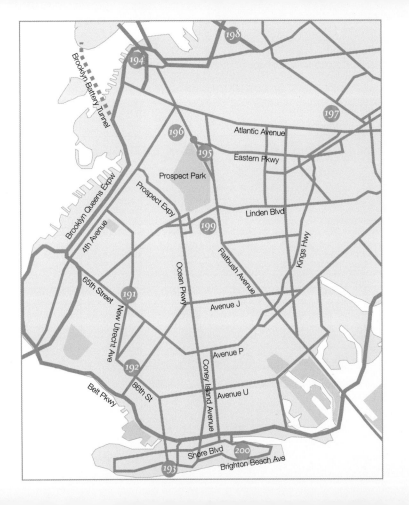

BROOKLYN

191 THE FRENCH CONNECTION (1971)
62nd Street and New Utrecht Avenue Station
Nicoli hijacks a train and Popeye chases him in a car, then shoots him when he attempts to escape.

192 SATURDAY NIGHT FEVER (1977)
86th Street, Bensonhurst
Tony struts down 86th Street to the Bee Gees' song, "Stayin' Alive" and gets himself a pair of slices at Lenny's Pizza.

193 UPTOWN GIRLS (2003)
Coney Island
When Ray's father dies, Molly finds Ray in Coney Island riding a giant teacup and she collapses into Molly's arms.

194 MOONSTRUCK (1987)
Loretta's House: 19 Cranberry Street
After Johnny cancels the engagement, Ronny takes the ring from his brother and asks Loretta to marry him; she accepts.

195 THE ONLY LIVING BOY IN NEW YORK (2017) *Brooklyn Museum: 200 Eastern Parkway*
Thomas surprises Johanna, his father's mistress, with a kiss at the party at the museum, and they begin an affair.

196 MONA LISA SMILE (2003)
St. Augustine Catholic Church: 116 Sixth Avenue
Katherine is invited to Betty's lavish wedding but within six months her marriage falls apart because of Spencer's affair.

197 DO THE RIGHT THING (1989)
Sal's Famous Pizzeria: Lexington and Stuyvesant Avenues
The pizzeria owner's refusal to change the Wall of Fame leads to tragic violence in the Bedford-Stuyvesant community.

198 COMING TO AMERICA (1988)
Prince Akeem's Apartment: 390 South 5th Street
After driving from JFK airport, Akeem and Semmi step out of the cab into "the most common part of Queens."

199 SOPHIE'S CHOICE (1982)
The "Pink Palace" Boarding House: 101 Rugby Road
Stingo, a young writer, moves to Brooklyn and befriends Sophie and Nathan at a rooming house, the "Pink Palace."

200 TWO LOVERS (2008)
Brighton Beach
Distraught, Leonard heads out to the beach, and as he drops a glove Sandra gave him, he realizes that she loves him.

LOST NEW YORK . . .

Copacabana on 60th Street in
GOODFELLAS (1990)
Original Penn Station in
KILLER'S KISS (1955)
Twin Towers in KING KONG (1976)
CBGB in SUMMER OF SAM (1999)

Subway graffiti in SATURDAY NIGHT FEVER (1977)
Tenement buildings on West 68th Street in WEST SIDE
STORY (1990)

Film Index

PHOTO CREDIT

PAGE 4: KING KONG (1933), ©RKO PICTURES. PAGE 8: BREAKFAST AT TIFFANY'S (1961), GEORGE PEPPARD, AUDREY HEPBURN, PHOTO BY KEYSTONE FEATURES/ GETTY IMAGES ©PARAMOUNT. PAGE 11: SCENT OF A WOMAN (1992), GABRIELLE ANWAR, AL PACINO, ©UNIVERSAL. PAGE 13: SERENDIPITY (2001), KATE BECKINSALE, JOHN CUSACK, ©MIRAMAX. PAGE 15: ANNIE HALL (1977), DIANE KEATON, WOODY ALLEN, ©MGM. PAGE 17: MIDNIGHT COWBOY (1969), JON VOIGHT, SYLVIA MILES, ©MGM. PAGE 19: THE THOMAS CROWN AFFAIR (1968), PIERCE BROSNAN, PHOTO BY MARY EVANS/RONALD GRANT. PAGE 21: OCEAN'S EIGHT (2018), HELENA BONHAM CARTER, PHOTO BY BARRY WETCHER, ©WARNER BROS; GOSSIP GIRL (2007-2012), BLAKE LIVELY, ©WARNER BROTHERS; MR. POPPER'S PENGUINS (2011), ©2011 TWENTIETH CENTURY FOX. PAGE 23: THE INTERNATIONAL (2009), CLIVE OWEN, DIRECTOR TOM TYKWER, ©COLUMBIA PICTURES. PAGE 26: BREAKFAST AT TIFFANY'S (1961), GEORGE PEPPARD, AUDREY HEPBURN, ©PARAMOUNT; THE SEVEN YEAR ITCH (1955), MARILYN MONROE, ©20TH CENTURY FOX FILM CORP; 25TH HOUR (2002), BARRY PEPPER, PHILIP SEYMOUR HOFFMAN, EDWARD NORTON, ©WALT DISNEY; BUTTERFIELD 8 (1960), ELIZABETH TAYLOR. PAGE 28: THE APRIL FOOLS (1969), JACK LEMMON, CATHERINE DENEUVE. PAGE 31: DEFINITELY, MAYBE (2008), RYAN REYNOLDS, ELIZABETH BANKS, PHOTO BY MARY EVANS, ©UNIVERSAL STUDIOS. PAGE 33: KRAMER VS. KRAMER (1979), JUSTIN HENRY, DUSTIN HOFFMAN, ©COLUMBIA PICTURES. PAGE 34: WHEN HARRY MET SALLY... (1989), MEG RYAN, BILLY CRYSTAL, ©COLUMBIA PICTURES. PAGE 35: SERENDIPITY (2001), KATE BECKINSALE, JOHN CUSACK, ©MIRAMAX; FRIENDS WITH BENEFITS (2011), JUSTIN TIMBERLAKE, MILA KUNIS, PHOTO BY GLEN WILSON, ©SCREEN GEMS; IT SHOULD HAPPEN TO YOU (1954), JACK LEMMON, JUDY HOLLIDAY, ©SONY PICTURES; THE AVENGERS (2012), ©WALT DISNEY STUDIOS. PAGE 37: IT COULD HAPPEN TO YOU (1994), NICOLAS CAGE, BRIDGET FONDA, ©TRISTAR. PAGE 39: CAFÉ SOCIETY (2016), JESSE EISENBERG, KRISTEN STEWART, WOODY ALLEN, ©LIONSGATE. PAGE 42: MADAGASCAR (2005), ©DREAMWORKS; MARATHON MAN (1976), DUSTIN HOFFMAN, ©PARAMOUNT PICTURES; LOVE STORY (1970), RYAN O'NEAL, ALI MACGRAW, ©PARAMOUNT PICTURES. PAGE 43: THE PRODUCERS (2005), MATTHEW BRODERICK NATHAN LANE, ©UNIVERSAL STUDIOS. PAGE 44: THE APARTMENT (1960), JACK LEMON, ©MGM.

PAGE 47: GHOSTBUSTERS (1984), ©SONY PICTURES. PAGE 49: CROCODILE DUNDEE (1986), PAUL HOGAN, ©PARAMOUNT PICTURES. PAGE 51: MOONSTRUCK (1987), NICOLAS CAGE, CHER, ©MGM. PAGE 53: BLACK SWAN (2010), VINCENT CASSEL, NATALIE PORTMAN, ©FOX SEARCHLIGHT; GOSSIP GIRL (2007-2012), SAM PAGE, LEIGHTON MEESTER, GILLIAN MURPHY, ETHAN STIEFEL, BLAKE LIVELY, PHOTO BY GIOVANNI RUFINO/WARNER BROTHERS TELEVISION; JOHN WICK, CHAPTER TWO (2017), KEANU REEVES, ©LIONSGATE; FOCUS (2015), WILL SMITH, MARGOT ROBBIE, PHOTO BY FRANK MASI/©WARNER BROS. PAGE 55: ROSEMARY'S BABY (1987), JOHN CASSAVETES & MIA FARROW, ©PARAMOUNT PICTURES. PAGE 57: SINGLE WHITE FEMALE (1992), JENNIFER JASON LEIGH, BRIDGET FONDA, ©SONY PICTURES. PAGE 59: YOU'VE GOT MAIL (1998), TOM HANKS, MEG RYAN, ©WARNER BROTHERS. PAGE 61: NIGHT AT THE MUSEUM (2006), BEN STILLER, 2006, ©20TH CENTURY FOX. PAGE 64: GHOSTBUSTERS (1984), DAN AYKROYD, BILL MURRAY, HAROLD RAMIS, ERNIE HUDSON, ©COLUMBIA PICTURES; YOU'VE GOT MAIL (1998), TOM HANKS, MEG RYAN, ©WARNER BROTHERS; SEX AND THE CITY (1998-2004), SARAH JESSICA PARKER, JOHN CORBETT, ©HBO; KISSING JESSICA STEIN (2001), JENNIFER WESTFELDT, HEATHER JUERGENSEN, ©FOX SEARCHLIGHT PICTURES; GREEN CARD (1990), GÉRARD DEPARDIEU, ANDIE MACDOWELL, ©WALT DISNEY. PAGE 67: KLUTE (1971), DONALD SUTHERLAND, JANE FONDA, ©WARNER BROTHERS. PAGE 69: WEST SIDE STORY (1961), GEORGE CHAKIRIS, RUSS TAMBLYN, DAVID WINTERS, ©MGM, PAGE 71: MALCOLM X (1992), DENZEL WASHINGTON, ©WARNER BROS. PAGE 74: SEINFELD (1990-1998), JERRY SEINFELD, JULIA LOUIS-DREYFUS, MICHAEL RICHARDS, JASON ALEXANDER, ©SONY PICTURES; THE LAST SEDUCTION (1994), BILL PULLMAN, LINDA FIORENTINO, ©NEW VIDEO GROUP. PAGE 75: AMERICAN GANGSTER (2007), RUSSELL CROWE, DENZEL WASHINGTON, ©UNIVERSAL; THE ROYAL TENENBAUMS (2001), LUKE WILSON, GWYNETH PALTROW, GENE HACKMAN, BEN STILLER, ANJELICA HUSTON, DANNY GLOVER, KUMAR PALLANA, GRANT ROSENMEYER, JONAH MEYERSON, ©TOUCHSTONE PICTURES; JUNGLE FEVER (1991), WESLEY SNIPES, VERONICA TIMBERS, ©UNIVERSAL. PAGE 77: HOW TO MARRY A MILLIONAIRE (1953), MARILYN MONROE, BETTY GRABLE, LAUREN BACALL, ©20TH CENTURY FOX. PAGE 79: THE FISHER KING (1991), GRAND CENTRAL STATION, ©SONY PICTURES. PAGE 81: THE GIRL ON THE TRAIN (2016), EMILY BLUNT, ©UNIVERSAL; ARTHUR (2011), RUSSELL BRAND, GRETA GERWIG, ©WARNER BROS; NORTH BY NORTHWEST (1959), CARY GRANT, ©WARNER BROS. PAGE 83: THE INTERPRETER (2005), SEAN PENN, ©UNIVERSAL. PAGE 85: THE SEVEN YEAR ITCH (1955), MARILYN MONROE, TOM

EWELL, © 20TH CENTURY FOX. *PAGE 87:* BREAKFAST AT TIFFANY'S (1961), AUDREY HEPBURN, © PARAMOUNT PICTURES. *PAGE 89:* BIG (1988), ROBERT LOGGIA, TOM HANKS, ©20TH CENTURY FOX. *PAGE 91:* MANHATTAN (1979), DIANE KEATON, WOODY ALLEN, ©MGM. *PAGE 93:* SPIDER-MAN (2002), TOBEY MAGUIRE, KIRSTEN DUNST, © SONY PICTURES; THE DARK KNIGHT RISES (2012), JOSEPH GORDON-LEVITT, PHOTO BY RON PHILLIPS, © WARNER BROS; A MOST VIOLENT YEAR (2014), J.C. CHANDOR, ©A24STUDIO; SALT (2010), ANGELINA JOLIE, ©COLUMBIA PICTURES. *PAGE 96:* MAN ON A LEDGE (2012), JAMIE BELL, ELIZABETH BANKS, PHOTO BY MYLES ARONOWITZ, © SUMMIT; GOSSIP GIRL (2007-2012), BLAKE LIVELY, CHACE CRAWFORD, © WARNER BROS; THE LOST WEEKEND (1945), RAY MILLAND, HOWARD DA SILVA, © UNIVERSAL; THE DEVIL WEARS PRADA (2006), ANNE HATHAWAY, ©20TH CENTURY FOX. *PAGE 98:* AN AFFAIR TO REMEMBER (1957), CARY GRANT, DEBORAH KERR, ©20TH CENTURY FOX. *PAGE 101:* SLEEPLESS IN SEATTLE (1993), MEG RYAN, ROSS MALINGER, TOM HANKS, ©TRISTAR PICTURES. *PAGE 103:* MIRACLE ON 34TH STREET (1947), NATALIE WOOD, JOHN PAYNE, ©20TH CENTURY FOX. *PAGE 105:* SEX AND THE CITY: THE MOVIE, CYNTHIA NIXON, KRISTIN DAVIS, SARAH JESSICA PARKER, KIM CATTRALL, 2008. © NEW LINE CINEMA. *PAGE 107:* ONE FINE DAY (1996), MAE WHITMAN, GEORGE CLOONEY, ALEX D. LINZ, MICHELLE PFEIFFER, ©20TH CENTURY FOX. *PAGE 109:* BIRDMAN OR (THE UNEXPECTED VIRTUE OF IGNORANCE) (2014), MICHAEL KEATON, EDWARD NORTON, ©20TH CENTURY FOX. *PAGE 111:* : VANILLA SKY (2001), TOM CRUISE, PENÉLOPE CRUZ, © PARAMOUNT PICTURES. *PAGE 112:* ENCHANTED (2007), AMY ADAMS, © BUENA VISTA PICTURES. *PAGE 113:* STAYING ALIVE (1983), JOHN TRAVOLTA, © PARAMOUNT PICTURES; CROCODILE DUNDEE (1986), PAUL HOGAN, © PARAMOUNT PICTURES; NOW YOU SEE ME (2013), ISLA FISHER, JESSE EISENBERG, WOODY HARRELSON, © SUMMIT ENTERTAINMENT; 13 GOING ON 30 (2004), JENNIFER GARNER, © SONY PICTURES. *PAGE 115:* TAXI DRIVER (1976), ROBERT DENIRO, © COLUMBIA PICTURES. *PAGE 117:* 30 ROCK (2006-2013), TRACY MORGAN, RACHEL DRATCH, JACK MCBRAYER, TINA FEY, ALEC BALDWIN, PHOTO BY MITCHELL HAASETH, © NBC. *PAGE 119:* MANHATTAN (1979), WOODY ALLEN, DIANE KEATON, ©MGM. *PAGE 121:* SEINFELD (1989-1998), JULIA LOUIS-DREYFUS, LARRY THOMAS AS THE SOUP NAZI, © COLUMBIA TRISTAR TELEVISION. *PAGE 123:* MIDNIGHT COWBOY (1969), JON VOIGHT, DUSTIN HOFFMAN, ©MGM. *PAGE 125:* LEON; THE PROFESSIONAL, NATALIE PORTMAN, JEAN RENO, © SONY PICTURES. *PAGE 127:* HOME ALONE 2 (1992), MACAULAY CULKIN, JOE PESCI, DANIEL STERN, © 20TH CENTURY FOX. *PAGE 130:* HOW TO LOSE A GUY IN 10 DAYS (2003), MATTHEW MCCONAUGHEY, KATE HUDSON, © PARAMOUNT PICTURES; LETTERS TO JULIET (2010), AMANDA SEYFRIED, © SUMMIT ENTERTAINMENT; TOOTSIE (1982), DUSTIN HOFFMAN, JESSICA LANGE, © SONY PICTURES; FAME, (1980), © TURNER ENTERTAINMENT. *PAGE 132:* THE ADJUSTMENT BUREAU (2012), MATT DAMON, EMILY BLUNT, © UNIVERSAL; SEX AND THE CITY 2 (2010), CYNTHIA NIXON, SARAH JESSICA PARKER, KRISTIN DAVIS, PHOTO BY CRAIG BLANKENHORN, © WARNER BROS; SWEET SMELL OF SUCCESS (1957), TONY CURTIS, BURT LANCASTER, ©MGM. *PAGE 134:* REAR WINDOW (1954), GRACE KELLY, JAMES STEWART, © PARAMOUNT PICTURES. *PAGE 137:* THE AGE OF INNOCENCE (1993), WINONA RYDER, DANIEL DAY-LEWIS, © COLUMBIA PICTURES. *PAGE 139:* ACROSS THE UNIVERSE (2007), MARTIN LUTHER, DANA FUCHS, JOE ANDERSON, © SONY PICTURES. *PAGE 141:* THE HOURS (2002), MERYL STREEP, © PARAMOUNT. *PAGE 143:* AS GOOD AS IT GETS (1997), HELEN HUNT, JACK NICHOLSON, GREG KINNEAR, © TRISTAR PICTURES. *PAGE 145:* FRIENDS (1994-2004) "SERIES FINALE", MATTHEW PERRY, LISA KUDROW, DAVID SCHWIMMER, COURTENEY COX ARQUETTE, JENNIFER ANISTON, MATT LEBLANC, © WARNER BROS. *PAGE 147:* AUGUST RUSH (2007), JONATHAN RHYS MEYERS, FREDDIE HIGHMORE, © WARNER BROS. *PAGE 148:* DON JON (2013): JOSEPH GORDON-LEVITT, JULIANNE MOORE, © RELATIVITY MEDIA. *PAGE 149:* BAREFOOT IN THE PARK (1967), ROBERT REDFORD, © PARAMOUNT PICTURES; INSIDE LLEWYN DAVIS (2013), OSCAR ISAAC, © SONY PICTURES; WHEN HARRY MET SALLY... (1989), MEG RYAN, BILLY CRYSTAL, 1989, © COLUMBIA; SEARCHING FOR BOBBY FISCHER (1993), LAURENCE FISHBURNE, MAX POMERANC, © PARAMOUNT PICTURES. *PAGE 151:* SEX AND THE CITY (1998-2004), SARAH JESSICA PARKER, JOHN CORBETT, © HBO. *PAGE 154:* SERENDIPITY (2001), KATE BECKINSALE, © MIRAMAX; SLEEPERS (1996), BILLY CRUDUP, BRAD PITT, JASON PATRIC, RON ELDARD, © WARNER BROS; NEXT STOP, GREENWICH VILLAGE (1976), LENNY BAKER, CHRISTOPHER WALKEN, ELLEN GREENE, ANTONIO FARGAS, DORI BRENNER, ©20TH CENTURY FOX; MO' BETTER BLUES (1990), SPIKE LEE, © UNIVERSAL; ALMOST FAMOUS (2000), PATRICK FUGIT, KATE HUDSON, © PARAMOUNT PICTURES. *PAGE 156:* SEX AND THE CITY (1998–2004): CYNTHIA NIXON, SARAH JESSICA PARKER, © HBO; SEX AND THE CITY (1998–2004): SARAH JESSICA PARKER, KIM CATTRALL, © HBO; SEX AND THE CITY (1998–2004): CYNTHIA NIXON, DAVID EIGENBERG, © HBO; SEX AND THE CITY (2008): EVAN HANDLER, JASON LEWIS, CHRIS NOTH, DAVID EIGENBERG, © NEW LINE. *PAGE 158:* THE FRENCH CONNECTION (1971), WILLIAM FRIEDKIN, GENE HACKMAN, ROY SCHEIDER, ©20TH CENTURY FOX. *PAGE 161:* GREAT EXPECTATIONS (1998), ETHAN HAWKE,

Gwyneth Paltrow, Director Alfonso Cuaron, 1998. © 20th Century Fox. **Page 163:** The Godfather: Part II (1974), Robert De Niro, © Paramount Pictures. **Page 165:** When Harry Met Sally... (1989), Meg Ryan, Billy Crystal, © Columbia Pictures. **Page 167:** Eternal Sunshine Of The Spotless Mind (2004), Jim Carrey, © Focus Features. **Page 169:** P.S. I Love You (2007), Hilary Swank, © Warner Bros. **Page 171:** The Godfather Part III (1990), Joe Mantegna, Andy Garcia, © Paramount Pictures. **Page 173:** The Godfather (1972), Marlon Brando, John Cazale, © Paramount Pictures. **Page 176:** Taxi Driver (1976), Jodie Foster, © Sony Pictures; The Naked City (1948), © Universal; Donnie Brasco (1997), Johnny Depp, © Tristar. **Page 178 and 181:** Ghost (1990), Demi Moore, Patrick Swayze, © Paramount Pictures. **Page 183:** Unfaithful (2002), Diane Lane, ©20th Century Fox, Courtesy Of Getty Images. **Page 185:** Ghostbusters (1984), Bill Murray, Dan Aykroyd, Harold Ramis, © Columbia Pictures. **Page 188:** Hitch (2005), Will Smith, Eva Mendes, © Columbia Pictures; 9 1/2 Weeks (1986), Kim Basinger, © Warner Bros. **Page 189:** Basquiat (1996), Jeffrey Wright, David Bowie, © Miramax, Sex And The City (1998–2004): Cynthia Nixon, Sarah Jessica Parker, Kim Cattrall, Kristin Davis, © HBO. **Page 191:** On The Town (1949), Jules Munshin, Frank Sinatra, Gene Kelly, © Warner Bros. **Page 193:** Gangs Of New York (2002), Daniel Day-Lewis, © Miramax. **Page 195:** Kate & Leopold (2001), © Miramax, Courtesy Of Getty Images. **Page : 196:** Mo' Better Blues (1990), Denzel Washington, © Universal. **Page 197:** Wolfen (1981), © Warner Bros; Kate and Leopold (2001), Meg Ryan, © Miramax; John Wick: Chapter Two (2017), Keanu Reeves, © Summit Entertainment; Sex And The City (2008), Cynthia Nixon, © New Line. **Page 199:** I Am Legend (2007), Will Smith, © Warner Bros. **Page 201:** 13 Going On 30 (2004), Jennifer Garner, Mark Ruffalo, © Columbia Pictures. **Page 203:** Once Upon A Time In America (1984), © Warner Bros. **Page 205:** The Dark Night Rises (2012), Tom Hardy, Christian Bale, © Warner Bros. **Page 207:** Inside Man (2006), Denzel Washington, Director Spike Lee, © Universal. **Page 208:** Crocodile Dundee II (1988), Paul Hogan, © Paramount Pictures. **Page 209:** Sabrina (1954), Audrey Hepburn, William Holden, © Paramount Pictures; The Devil's Advocate (1997), Keanu Reeves, Al Pacino, © Warner Bros; The Apartment (1960), Jack Lemon, © MGM; Wall Street (1987), Michael Douglas, © 20th Century Fox. **Page 211:** Desperately Seeking Susan (1985), Robert Joy, Madonna, © Orion. **Page 213:** Working Girl (1988), Melanie Griffith, © 20th Century Fox. **Page 215:** Ghostbusters II (1989), Bill Murray, Ernie Hudson, Dan Aykroyd, Harold Ramis, © Columbia Pictures. **Page 218:** The Wolf Of Wall Street (2013), Ted Griffin, Leonardo DiCaprio, Kyle Chandler photo by Mary Cybulski, © Paramount Pictures; Anger Management (2003), Adam Sandler, Jack Nicholson, © Columbia Pictures; Annie Hall (1977), Diane Keaton, Woody Allen, © MGM. **Page 220:** Serpico (1973), Al Pacino, © Paramount Pictures. **Page 223:** The French Connection (1971), Gene Hackman, Marcel Bozzuffi, © 20th Century Fox. **Page 225:** Saturday Night Fever (1977), John Travolta, © Paramount Pictures. **Page 227:** Uptown Girls (2003), Brittany Murphy, Dakota Fanning, © MGM. **Page 229:** Wonder Wheel (2017), Juno Temple, photo by Atsushi Nishijima, © Amazon; The Warriors (1979), Tom McKitterick, Marcellino Sanchez, David Harris, Michael Beck, Deborah Van Valkenburgh, Brian Tyler, © Paramount Pictures; Requiem For A Dream (2000), Jared Leto, © Artisan Entertainment; Brooklyn (2015), Emory Cohen, Saoirse Ronan, photo by Kerry Brow, © Fox Searchlight. **Page 232:** Moonstruck (1987), Vincent Gardenia, Cher, Nicolas Cage, © MGM; Do The Right Thing (1989), Spike Lee, © Universal; Coming to America (1988), Eddie Murphy, © Paramount Pictures; The Only Living Boy In New York (2017), Kate Beckinsale, Callum Turner, photo by Niko Tavernise, © Lionsgate. **Page 233:** Sophie's Choice (1982), Kevin Kline, Meryl Streep, Peter Macnicol, © Universal; Two Lovers (2008), Vinessa Shaw, Joaquin Phoenix, © Magnolia Pictures. **Page 234:** Goodfellas (1990), Ray Liotta, Joe Pesci, Frank Sivero, © Warner Bros; Killer's Kiss (1955), Jamie Smith, © MGM; King Kong (1976), © Paramount Pictures; Summer Of Sam (1999), Mira Sorvino, John Leguizamo, © Walt Disney. **Page 235:** Saturday Night Fever (1977), John Travolta, © Paramount Pictures; West Side Story(1961), George Chakiris (Center), © MGM.

MUSEYON INC.
333 East 45th Street, New York, NY 10017
museyon.com
instagram.com/museyonbooks
facebook.com/museyon
twitter.com/museyon
info@museyon.com

ABOUT THE AUTHOR

Alex Child has lived in New York since 1987. After managing a movie and TV licensing business he has worked on publishing projects including Film+Travel Europe; Film+Travel Asia, Oceania, Africa; Film+Travel North America, South America; and Art+Travel Europe.